Firewriting
& Other Poems

Also by John Muckle:

Poetry
It Is Now As It Was Then (with Ian Davidson)
Firewriting (online at www.shearsman.com)

Prose
The Cresta Run
Bikers (with Bill Griffiths)
Cyclomotors

As General Editor:
The New British Poetry (eds., Allnutt, D'Aguiar, Edwards, Mottram)

Firewriting

& other poems

John Muckle

Shearsman Books
Exeter

First published in the United Kingdom in 2005 by
Shearsman Books Ltd
58 Velwell Road
Exeter EX4 4LD

http://www.shearsman.com/

ISBN 0-907562-64-7

Acknowledgements

Some of these poems have previously appeared in the following publications,
often in earlier versions.

CCCP Handbook, GreatWorks, Jacket, Poetry Salzburg, PN Review, Shearsman and
Birthday Boy: A Present for Lee Harwood (Ship of Fools, 1999) and *For Tom and Val*
(Pressed Wafer, 2004).

The author wishes to thank the editors for their support.

CONTENTS

1

"How continually it comes to pass, thought Hepzibah, in this dull delirium of a world, — that whosoever, and with however kindly a purpose, should come to help, they would be sure to help the strongest side. Might and wrong combined, like iron magnetized, are endowed with irresistible attraction."

Nathaniel Hawthorne, *The House of the Seven Gables*

1

CARING FOR YOU

My new job takes up more of my waking days
But sometimes it seems an easy, useful thing to do
Arriving to find Shane already up & risen
Shouting to be washed. In your letter, good news
Of a vocation! I really like the way you write.

And, seeing I am wet through from cycling
Steve finds a dry pair of jeans, same colour,
In his wardrobe drawer. What's he saying?
Not much probably, enough for now, just enough.
Alright, John? I've been good. I've been good for you.
I put wet things in the hall airing cupboard
And wipe Shane over with a half-damp flannel.

Mad Darren the master tea-leaf is at it again.
He hovers at my shoulder by an open padlock
Feathering hands at the edge of peripheral vision
Tossing up leaves to watch them blow away,
Sidles in like a cat burglar for the jar of QT.
A mid-morning decaff is his methadone.

And I feel as though someone had set me a test
As we listen to a crackly single, to its flipside:
Come on and take the rest of me, you know it?
The Real Thing, circa the year you were born.
My hearing both present and a late reminder
Of what came before us, which is far too much.

On nights – ginger-haired Lauren in the lounge –
And I sleep on through Shane's fits and diarrhoea
But at least I can spell it rightly in the morning.
Fran and Lauren are scrubbing out the carpet.
They love it, that's my explanation. Poor Shane
Shaking, sobbing, disorientated and ashamed.
All men are fated similarly. No choice, you let them

Irene does her backward vocal clicks – gibbering her
yadayadaya. Be quiet. Rubs her head, her knee.
And lays her curly head in my lap. All better now.

Life's flickering. I've got seven women on my mind
Growing like tuberous sclerosis, white larvae in my brain.
In the hall, in the back garden. Blearily singing.

IN A LONELY PLACE

I cried and sang, seeing only what was awful to see.
Everything as empty as a face whose own light
Is left broken or helplessly replaced
By rays from a surrogate sun. That cracked me wide open
And all fun yellowed and seemed to mock at me . . .

It had turned blue, but obscenely
As though each morning bore a new death by slow stages
Another lapidary entry in the Unusual Occurrences Book.
Shane picked up an iron bar; Steven May
Struck out at kids, was quickly restrained on the beach
At Clacton, appalled in the knowledge of his malice.
Trying to run to safety in the off-white minibus.
A whole Shanedom to draw you into
As you opened your mouth around a pattern.

A book of lies not truth.
Yes. Each point is taken. Had I been deceived
By her openness, a crime, or a plan,
Or should I open a vein? Darren
Through the front window, straight next-door
Had helped himself to tea-bag. Such a lovely
Well-mannered boy. We made
Him a cup and a buttered bun.
Stayed here, very charming. We thought
He might miss his mother ... so gentle and affectionate ...
All orders calculated in advance, a charade
That swallowed up the world; chewed, but slightly
Lightly, and decided to spit it out on the mat.

Delighting inference of blame at Shane's late lie-in.
A blind-eye stared out ... you let him sleep too long.
Soap scum in the sink, records thrown about his room:
The things he plays with others put there for him.
Come on, I know so many people like that
And I try to guide & cajole this into being what it isn't.

The rights folder's cover. Her scheme of gargantuan squalor
Was growing daily to fruition; we're enthralled

By our complicity in the knowledge of darkness,
The way the leaves tear off, small scraps of pornography
Weathered in the rains. Another story circulates at lunch
In looks and glances; the old barter & exchange system
Of night, duplicity & silence. Oh, Mr Kennedy called
Hoping to destabilise the profit motive in an angry word.
Shane & a member of staff had been out watering the garden.

PITCH & FLOSS

To speak it out in an anecdote
When it won't do or be as story
A blocked way that is used up
Some of people live by stories
Some people give off signals

A view seen from a window
And here below is what has occurred
No way or circling quest

No news of a far death
Nor traveller's library of received wisdom

You unlock a cupboard
They are ready and waiting

Dear Floss has nothing to tell
Her last candle
                    stubbed out

Andrew paces you on the balls of his feet
A green coat prompting alarm in his erections
The signal to unwind him
Derives from a technique of interviewers
What does Terri do (Terri Tomato)
Imitates their fits (repeats songs and catchphrases)
And leaving a slight gap for absent remembered people
Who have vanished for the day to Colchester or to the coast
Suspended in amber, his mind reposes.
Quite the conformist, a true coward
Creaking like a rusty machine
Recalling in a sequence of actions or gestures
Performed in a species of dream
Pulled out of an empty sack, no-one's home
Returns to another dream
& invents the glass thimble

So you feel sorry, you can
They will never see you properly, only say

Your words in drips and dribbles
Altering without doubt

        Your meaning
Nowhere left to go
A nothing comes to pass
A pasteboard counter

Smiles at another's ordeal
Letting go one of his mock rages
A pleasure in his sister's pain
Readily cracks his face

Girl fears are unspoken
Wondering where they have gone
Obeys commands
Nobody rushes towards a knife

Trying to find a word for you
What isn't black or candy
Boy or girl, lightness and darkness
Treacle set into a rock

On a small percentage, sad or happy
Now trying, now playing dumb
Gone where, gone there
Without rhyme or reason
Like a dropped stone in the grass

THRILLING WONDER STORIES

I'd like to write a few of those myself.

★

The sheen of them, so and so's shy smile.

★

Care's An Easy Living.

★

Space 1999: Between Your Ears.

MAKING IT

"Art is medicine for imbeciles" — Ted Berrigan

"Who is going to work with Irene?"
Everybody demurs, the air's thick with protestations,
Tantrums, claws appear – and Irene is plumped
Down at one of the round tables. "John," says Sam,
"Would you like to work with Irene today?"

I don't say anything, not wanting to seem eager
Or crawl. Pick some clean white cards, markers,
Pencils, stencils, shout her down, shove
A red pen in her hand, and set her to draw
Hoping the miracle of Monday daycare will occur.

Irene is right there, stabbing me with her pen,
Scribbling a violent square with cross-hatched bars.
White teeth are pulled to gums, an excited screech.
I switch the red to mauve and cobalt blue
And it's a reasonable start. Broken everywhere, spluttering
Like a damp bonfire with petrol underneath

Her lines crackle and fizz. I grab the stencil
Snatch a blue felt-tip from her fist and write
Irene Irene Goodnight. 26. Nininini. An eggshell, a heart, an arrow –
All a bit Tracey Emin, if you know what I mean,
And we finish up a whole cellophane packet of silver stars.

How quickly these hours wear on
Quiet, intense, encapsulated days
That might have been a lesson to her
Had she understood the words passed
Between us, like pencil and paper.

"What do you think would make Irene's life better?"
I enquire of Julian, who is sitting opposite Andrew
Painting a burnt match stick black with a modelling sable.
"A silver bullet," is what he mutters.
Another subject I wasn't meant to touch
Being new at this game and superficially impressive.

I know I will never forget these
First stumbling steps, remembering them in the way of inside and outside,
    up and down,
Early manoeuvres I'd hoped would cling to me –
But will Irene remember this day
Or see her own finished drawings piled up in a stack like fresh laundry?

Following tea break we pack up all
The materials in the day care trailer
And coax wobbly Steve into the back of the minibus, set off
On a short drive home to lunch –
Each looking out through a similar window,
A quintet of improvisers with no common repertoire.

We hate them so these creatures, they don't hate us
Their horizons are too limited, putting it mildly.
"It's cruel to keep them alive," says Julian as, adding cruelty to cruelty,
He pulls Irene's hair, screams in her face to "shut up!"
A troubled man, in love with a capricious woman;
I'd do the same to him if my opinions were worth anything.

Back in the kitchen she turns ten slices of toast
And microwaves four cans of Value Spaghetti –
A pseudo-aristocratic filly from a nineteenth-century novel
Bucking to feel the sting of Heathcliff's riding crop,
A small town flirt with too much time on her hands:
A headmaster's daughter, her name Stephanie.

Perhaps, though, Julian is right.
Andy's a machine on the blink
That should be turned off. These rights are a fiction
So we can have jobs. And beyond all this
For Joy and Alison to go on safari, and love it,
Returning to opine that Irene is a monkey.

Just trying to live in the world has a sinister ring.
Although others love it seems to make them unhappy
And I am as unhappy with this as anyone else.
It's only we who think of them, they can't see us;
They're in control yet cringe before our rule.

Needling for help, wheedling for attention,
Playing out their little dramas of malice when your back is turned,
Each twisting on his hook; a minnow shoal metaphor –
All of them jumping into your net, uninvited,
Quite impossible to gainsay or persuade to depart.

But I've resisted too many plain truths for too long
Although they've been set before me plainly enough;
I am stubborn. I wanted to believe in those things
Ubiquitous, free of charge: like a common cold
Unfolding in each of us, probably, in each of our hearts.

Irene's pictures aren't quite beautiful, or hers
Because it's me, really, who made them; and later
Julian tears them to bits in a jealous frenzy
Thinking I meant them as love notes to Princess Steph,
Empress of bathtime, bosses' nark. Okay, I like you,
          you scruffy tart,
But you're a silly mare, and such a careless madam.

I'm alright now. I'll be good. Look, I've got my pyjamas on. Look, I've got my jeans. I enjoyed that bath. I enjoyed that sleep. I enjoyed that dinner. I love you John. I love you Jamie. I love you Stephanie, you scruffy tart. Shut up madam. Shut up Shane Brown. You smelly arse. You fart in your pants, you do. Fuck off. Fuck off John. Fuck off Jamie. Beverley, fuck off. I'll be good now. I'm alright. I was a good boy. I was a good boy for you. Nokay not. Shut up. Get out of it. Clean my glasses. Wash my glasses. I can see now. Good. Will you help me John? I like Acorn. I like Joy. I like Alison. I like Michelle. I was good.

Were you good, Steve?
Yes, I was good.
Be good, Steve.
Why?

IT TAKES TWO LIPS OF FIRE

Steve's fluttering
His hands go crazy
                  like birds.
He twists his head
Wincing in a way that's not
Hurting exactly but a fear
Wondering when it will end
As fingers twitch and drum, short-circuited.
Will you take my glasses, please? Wash them?
All usual things.

Passes away in moments.
Enjoyed that dinner, that sleep, that med.
Bags by his chair in the lounge,
Laughter at the end of thought.

Got my jumper on now.
Got my jeans on look.
Cup of tea now, please.

Hair nestles over squareness
Does that he must
Jamie has stolen his nose
Give it back, Jamie, give it back, please.
Dinner in his room to protect the furniture
Turns over a laden table, unblinking.
Such a big one hurts
                  his sledgehammer
Hangs perpendicular
The weight of his life
Only to immerse in the water
Wondering if it might float.

TO MELT AWAY THE SNOW

What Steve likes
The way home. A good feed
No matter. All emotions are reversible
Forgets the last incident
A shaking leaf and vertigo.

In his room he stands
Hair wet in pyjamas
Holding up his crotch. Above all
Cautious, mildly asking you to turn off the light
A bath that has already happened.
Event order renegotiated
To bring him to this point: lay down and sleep.
A final nudge at the wall
Hoping the bugs won't bite
His whiskers. Whispering
Goodnight. Goodnight.

IT TAKES MORE THAN AN EFFORT

Extra hour at the end of a shift
Waiting for the doctor to arrive.
Comes and looks, a precise air
Asks a few vague questions
Steve nods quiet in a chair.
Can I go to bed now, please?
Catherine takes his pulse.
Big toe blistered and weeping.
Carpet burn. Hushed in the aftermath
Of seizure, convulsed and thrashed
Turned blue, paled. That doctor would not
Touch him, would not dare.

Getting sick of women
Explained but were afraid of him
Boldly I said that he was sweet
Talking to the doctor like this
Of, not about Steve
All reserve was dropped
Too well-educated to work here
Definitely not a trained nurse
And all of them. Typical
Behaviours. Of gender and class.
Touched his temple, put to bed.

IN DARREN'S ROOM

The boy smell's overpowering.
It's all messed up in minutes by the scraps of Shane's
Torn catalogue he flips before sly eyes:
A sign of intelligence, defined
As cunning. Alert & gazing raptly
In your face. Making his babababababa
To touch his parted lips, and yours,
Clutching your arm with his four-fingered hand
(He chewed off the smallest digit.)
Why is he so engaging, hair always mussed,
A prefab boy up to his mischief?
Yesterday he grabbed my hand
And pulled it down to his gaping fly.
I zipped him up quick.
Wouldn't want to try it too often
Caressing the semi-erect penis of a moron.
Moves like a cat, arching and prowling,
Hurls himself at walls, springs back,
Pivots, slaps his arse.
                              Kiss that.

I see him naked, strutting down the hall,
Drinking from a flannel, a cup,
A toilet brush holder. Filling a cold bath, tosses a salad,
Sits out on the lawn in his grey plastic
Over-trousers, runs in grinning with a muddy nose.
He grabs the wrist of a new girl, stares her down.
Darren certainly knows how to make them squeal,
Spreading his sandwich with a lick of the knife
With one shoe off & one shoe on, splayed
Toes of two left feet, the ruthless charm
Of the Wild Boy of Aveyron. Honks in pain, in fits
Retracts into himself, a flailing crab, a myoclonic jerk.
By the locked window he looks out at wet grass.
They gave him a cow's stomach by mistake
When assembling him from defective spare parts.

HANGING BY A THREAD, SWINGING ON A STAR

Samantha hangs her ring above my palm
on a swing, a hair. Spins clockwise,
      anticlockwise
          a yoyo at the end of its tether.
Twitches in several diagonals.
      A boy. A boy. Exchange glances. Yes.
Definitely a boy.
          One. One boy.

    ★

It takes a long time to find out
      that trouble is real.

It didn't take me long.

SO HARD TO FIND

Cup of tea? Supper? ... Oh, you're far too early
To be fed. And slides, the park's not open any more.
Nothing to look at.
Pain sundered even Steve's warm monotone.

Andrew starts an Elvis song and mercifully stops.
Dismembering a melody I had hoped would soon . . .
Why pretend to bother?
Slink around the windy streets of a dead town, appealing your fate.

Unkindly an obsessive phase would sometimes pop up.
The end of endowment. One of those lovely ballads.
And in my right hand a silver dagger. Chin up, chicken.
Nobody knows your what your destination is.

Pump of heartbeat, murmurations.
Women at play. Love is hooked to its shadow.
A place to make your stand. A long & winding way
Beyond traces or names, or letting a poor maiden so.

Clients' rolled socks
Around their beds at night. T-shirts, jeans, trainers,
Yesterday's underwear. Time is understood
To be pressing. And in its place

A restless period follows. After the med has been swallowed.

CARELESS LOVE

I've hurt others and I've hurt myself
And I blame no-one's remedy pushing out towards a far end.
Enchelia. Possibility. Of change. I've done some crappy things
In my prime, my time. And let me at it, I'll do them again.
Failure of a duty's borne, you begin over & make a start
On false names or worries. Unrelated to your particular life's
      woes and anxieties,
I know that. Jumping through hoops of fire for sex
Tenderness, concern. While sweet lust is lapping up milk.
The dice we rolled didn't improve us
Trying to see what you were, or did.
Obeying an instinct, sensing a mutual care.
All that hoping, hoping. Who will take up what I mean?
I'm watching emotions surge through us, break, wash & suck back
Temporary, yes, always revocable.
Looking into their eyes for a light, an answer. Seeing it.
Trading on the ignorance of the young.
Helping me write your book.
Helping you to write mine.
And I'm afraid there really is no light
Trying to get inside and to have you over
Rats' nests, dens of thieves – like me, like me.
All you despised: it's that simple.

Laughter
Indicative of indiscreet content
Knowing only the crap you have already created on this earth.
Power struggles, wars. Kiss the whip who wields it.
Throwing you a line to insist that you must
Make a special effort to be better
Than I am, really, insecure in my illusions of universal sympathy
In love with myself and things that grind you down.
It has caused me to weep. Vanity:
The cause and effect of love
Compacts of mutual back scratching.
It's a hard knock life when you tune into all that free radio
Drawing everything into a consideration of yourself
Inviting them in and holding them off with a counterplot
The absence of a steadying hand on your shoulder

And feminine wiles deployed by men
In search of an ongoing leg-over situation.
Moi aussi je serai un jour beau comme un dieu, and the bad guys offer up
The goods in a way, or seem to
And there's nothing much left to defend –
The path to sainthood leads through suicide
O plundering, taking & forgetting sky
Of how everything turned out to be so sordid.

HARMONIUM

O arrogant
my empty heart
blind man in a safe room

a keyboard is my light
one habit sticks
one tic has put me to the test

by rote, an upper console
oboes, clarinets –
each note a brick of light

I play for George to sing.
you can sing if you like
indifferent praise

of fairground waltzes, one-hand counterpoints
my shadow songs
from the child's hymnal of days.

It comes in shortened waves
each note a brick
a measured strophe of sun

wiped off the covers of a row of chairs
choked on a broken biscuit
stilled by shame.

Who wanted to be a bear.
Who hoped so much
that he and a bear would be friends –

a witch be his mother
a witch's brother
lover, friend

each tilted face
each nose a rose
each note a brick

I hold in place, set sail
atonic
apple of my eye

let loose –
O violets
red, blue.

KITCHENETTE

Basic instinct to betray others to authority.

★

Jason at the staff meeting. "He's such a woman."

★

Send Fouzi on an NVQ in oven management.

★

"I'd sack anyone else who said that."

LARGESSE

Ali
bestows a January sub
from the window of her people-carrier
smiles as you walk forward. A
misprint.
Expect errors on your timesheet
a nit-picker's charter is the norm
new rules with no explanation
or creative accounts?
a magnanimous role she likes to play
remembering earlier favours
imagined continents
move beneath her hand.

DRAFT BEER & WEENIES

Let me tell you about today's rumble.
Terry grabs Steve and holds him. All in fun
At first, but then not, because some bad imp
Gets hold of him, is there inside him all the time
Inviting strife and trying to hold it off.
String speed is a function of accuracy
Knowing which buttons to press. O seasons,
Castles, what soul is without blemish
And in what order to release the back gate
As Steve flipped out and struck him, hit out,
Today was wrestled to his room, ripped off
The handle, roaring, Terry, Terry, locks
Him in and takes his specs away. When did he start
To go or should I say who went, who went first?
Such is the view in each suburban bungalow
The magic study of happiness
Que nul n'élude. To wander naked
Each in his little world of violent tics
To say all men are brothers. And who
Will listen to my words or kiss
It better, or even confess to respecting me?
Can't pay, won't pay. I've tried to be patient
Admit I'm round the bend, yet misery
Drags after.
                    We're watching a video of Gene Vincent
On his last tour, playing some dive on the Isle of Wight
With the worst backing band in history. Terry
Hovers in the doorway. Shane perched
On the arm of my chair, slides into my lap.
At least I'm working with the best. He's
Great this bloke, he's really great. Do you know
Why he's dead? Cos he ate. He ate too much and drank
My tea. He looks like Michael Jackson, dunnee.
We've been waiting for you, Steve. By your door, bowing.
I'm alright now. Lead me to the nearest exit, please.
I'm glad you're feeling better. My heart's in Athens,
Texas ... Rome, Georgia ... and Paris, Tennessee.

AMBULANCE

for Bob Cobbing

Say a few words Shane. What do you want to say? Thankyou. I'll do it.
Hello Steve. Darling. Alright? I've been good. I was in my room. What?
There's Fran. I've got a scratch. Where? Oh, I see. I got a scratch. Look,
you can see it. Shht. Oeuur. Let's have a look. Who's that then? My mum.
Who's that? Who's the one next to her? Christopher. Darling darling. I
slipped this morning. In daycare. Thanks ouch done. Who else you got
there? Christopher. Look. Who else. Look, darling, it's Jonathan. Me.
You. My mum, look, look! Is that your dad? Yeah. Look, I've got one like
that, darling. Like what? At Mersea! Who else? Baby baby. Who's with the
baby? My mum. Let's have another one. Who's that? Car, car. Who's in
the car? Where's the car gone? Car look. Look car. Look, darling, look.
I've got one. Who's that with the hat on? Girl. Girl. Who's the girl? Look.
The ghost. The ghost, that is. That's the ghost. Boat. Boat. Look, boat
darling. You do it. Susan, who's Susan? Kumming. Kumming. Christopher.
Jonathan. They your brothers? They your brothers? Kumming! Kumming!
My dad look. Look, my mum. Look darling. Have a nice dinner Shane?
You've eaten it up, anyway. Jamie? Jamie? Jamie? Can I have some help,
please? Can't get all the little bits. Let's get all the little bits. Oh you've
gone a bit fluttery. Hello Irene. Ahdidididididididi. Mmmm. Eum. Yah. Yah.
Awebeh. Irene. All better. Commin hmm. Who's coming? Cup of tea.
Yes! Plis! Mmmhmmhm. Bequat. Teu. Hello darling. What do you want?
Nini. Dreeeeeeeeeeeeeeeeeee! Broka! Broka! Come here Shane. What do
you want? It's about a priest. Vestments. He has to have vestments. I think
it's... What does he do when he gets his vestments? What does he do? He
goes out. Yeah. And he goes in. And he sings he sings songs. Does he hold
his hands up? Sings songs. Then what does he do? What does he say? Play
guitars. Electric guitars. And does he hold his hands up in the air? Lord
forgive you. That's right. Also you. That's all. What else. Then he goes. He
says a lot of things though don't he. And he's gone. And he's gone. Tell us
what he says again. Lord forgive you. And the same to you. And he's gone.
I'm going to be a priest one day. When you get your vestments. Yeah. And
what'll you do when you're a priest? I get ... Drink your tea up then. No. No
more songs. What one's that? A different one. Umm. What? Yeah. What
song you talking bout? Morning has broken like the first morning. Ahahah
ahahaahyaayaayaa!Ahahah-h-h-hahahah! Ahanganananganananganagana
yanghehehehehehahaa. Anaynaynaynay. Go. Way. Go away. Ahhahaha
haha. Pardon? Bequat. Good girl. Be quiet. A yanayangayang. Eeeerna.

Commee. Aninininibebebebebebeneeneenee. Diedie. Wanya! Wanya! Ahh unh! Hnn. Morning like a first morning. That's what I said! Broad chordal strokes or lightning arpeggios does it. That's got morning has broken. What's an elephant and a digger? Combine harvester! What's in Africa and not in Africa? Guitars!

POINT CLEAR

A funny sort of day: to hold hands with Irene
On Point Clear beach, a look through weatherboard doors
At old ladies' ruminative knitting,
Crows, the sea wall, and an astounding
Ache. You bad girl,
Why didn't I humiliate you
Instead of letting you in to maul
My bag of threadbare broken tricks. A lapse, eh?
Steve tip-toes over each step and crack, gingerly
Into a muddy tide pool
Walking a tightrope beside the sea
As the earth's crust crumbles away
False-footing his last turn, and it's all
Remembering dreams of nasty kids, of searing
Chinese burns. My mother's light as driftwood.
I lift her, whimpering
And place her on a double bed
At home in the plenitude
Of penultimate days. I live here
And forget it, the outlying
Chalets peeled blue, and when will a smile not hide an ouch
Or an inflated frog?
No end to it, nor the hurt
I feel you're harbouring in your night fears
Spoken out to all and sundry,
Excited gabble in which you wish your life away.
It's just that you seemed as if I might
Be at least on the right ground
As turning to reassure Irene, she grunts, kicks out at me.
I grip her arm, stroke her knobby hand, shoulder her off,
Look over the water to Brightlingsea, at sixes and sevens.
Where's my window?
Am I getting better at this game of patience?
She settles into a steady shuffle and a honk
Of muted satisfaction, motion, my arm's pressure.
Results of passion: more bleating
A turn in the light
Towards darkness and blank dread
My crocodile shoes, where all

One sole is broken open to the seeping rains.
Thunder and pretentiousness amongst men.
Is that a hair or a pencil stroke
In the margin of the next day?
Sleep on it, night's misadventures, tidal rushings,
Bubbles pop in mud and moorings part company.
I mean to say, I mean
That dream is every dream
The point they're making is unclear
I'm back in the van
Thunder blue, or a scratch, with sea-salt rubbed in it.

SORRY

A big horse comes from a big bone
I'm talking about the yellow diggers
Shallow in affect, lacking in empathy
When things do not go my way.

Would you like a bath now?
I would like to have a bath.

Play my head on the shelf, play the fist on the me
Painful stimuli I am unable to master
Noises unbearably loud
Smells overpowering, people unpredictable & strange.

All my enemies. A problem of animate beings.
Given to outbursts, flattening, unable to account
Or say why. Faces loom & are forgotten.
Who what where. From I to thou I turn a page.

Preferring familiar arrangements, nor holding
A single thought in mind and performing an unrelated task.
Echolalia. No relation of persons to speech-acts.
No recognitions. A gypsy brother on his tractor
My strong and able provider. Who passes by.
Seeking magic and weapons

To destroy the monsters of earth.
No growing life behind these lines:
My failure to discern a false-belief
Quite frequent, easily tagged. An uncontrollable rage.

IBUPROFEN

Shane in his helmet & bubble anorak
an uncharged paintbrush in his left hand
stumbles to the ladder by the back gate
looking in the shed for a missing component
Rear light, hammer, hubcap
         & front wheel.
Steve gallops, biting the side of his hand
         on the hall chair, to his bed, to
            the hall chair.
Clacton Road traffic. A tree of sprouts
by the kitchen door.

            Darren heaps grass
on a binliner, grins at his reflection
in my grey-blue eyes
Philip's in the laundry room, folding
Oh when will Joy & Alison come
Back with Irene in the station wagon
Or Darren's med cocktail wear off
Throwing grass up against a white wall
beside the dustbins
          slapping his knee
& burbling in that rapt, purposeful way.

Power, Snow & Freedom.

Shane's toolbox. What you doing? Come
out of there or you'll fall on the bike
        & have your eye out. I'm doing
         a tractor.
Shaking by the barbeque, painting :
wrapping an extension flex around his
         palm & elbow.
Helping, clasping his hands together
      & laughing like a monk.

They have found a cure for toothache.

CODA

On a long two to nine with her & Jamie
She's doing the Gazette's crossword at the counter
Associating, trying to fit words in
To make them mesh up, slot together
Another low-grade word kit. She can't do it
& I try to help, gently pulling words
Out of her to see where they'll go.
I look at the cryptic clues & get a few right off.
But soon we're both struggling.
I'm like that still, don't like to stand out too far
Will fail under a sceptical gaze
Or prosper if someone believes in me. It's all crap
To me, she says, I don't get that at all.
It's easy when you know how, Tracy.
The Whole Thing Spoken In Anger To A Friend
I write in the gutter. That's like us the other day
She says. Are we friends? Yeah, if you say so.
I point to each word group with the tip of a pen.
Complete Crossword Companion. Oh yeah,
She says & smiles up at me, a nice big one. That's brilliant!
I wouldn't mind giving you a cuddle right now.
I'd want a bit more than that, John.
I'm standing behind her in the lounge doorway
As she gazes upwards at the mounted TV
Twitches the curtain to one side occasionally
Looking out for the headlights of Mr B.
Smiles over her shoulder as she feels my look:
Her eye-beams lasers to my central looking system.

HELLO

Today I'm Jennifer
equine toby jug
jerk my head away
(another flying fish)

people were good at making people laugh
people were good at making things

quiet in her chair by the window
straight-back on her walk-a-lator

whis-whis-whis
behind her hand
                        eyes of a what
this way
            & that

Stubborn, pliant as a girl's, his hands
turn easily, split melon face
a silent, slow-mo clap to one side
of head in shame, or bafflement.

His fingers crossed against what?
rocking from foot to foot
a wing-nut with a pudding bowl
asleep on his tongue's lollipop.

He chews a pale-blue singlet up
a velvet curtain's faded pink
hangs stiff with his dried spit
quacks on and on in Donald Duck

whilst straining fit to shit a brick.
You're lifting dead weight
strap him in the wheelchair
for a ride down the empty hall.

Take his left, he'll snatch it back
and give you right; right
and he'll offer left
if you don't mind a rote handshake

a groan, an uphill drag. I'd take his
wrists and pull him
palms against your sides, step back
to shift his centre; he'll follow

if you don't get into a fight –
a comfort drone of motor noise
of a sleepwalker; you back away
and draw him into the toilet tango.

EIGHT SONGS

1 Flux

Words.
I'll let them where they fall.
Soldered.
To words.
I wash one hand in misery & the other in milk.
Soldered.
To words!
Lone traveller. Deny it, play melodies.
Soldered.
Words.
The statutes tell
of a tide & a bright floor.
Of words.

2 Her Cries

The honey tasted so sweet
       on the end of the rod.
No wind blew through the house. Now
a sweet man tendered.
         Madness.
Now a bitter-sweet man tendered.
Even the sight was appalling, now gone
a dream lover spied over a bold stare.
       Now run
the honey tasted sweet, not on
the end of the rod, but ordered so.
A word blew through the house.

3 Table

    Uniforms & cycles.

Wild thorns
& short cries.

Oh they swear gruff
they demonstrate
by a lustrous word
by service of a plea
       mysteries.

    Uniforms & cycles.

A cry falls
on a flower.
What are these shouts of terror
celebrating the small forms?

     Spoils.
     All your harvest.

4 Unjust

Unjust.
Counterweights.
Juggle & reach, or
the one is the heavy one
light the wit of a truth.

To warn steep impact
a smile follows, world.

Unjust.
The bad seat.
Can't read: each one.

5 Born on a River

Namesake
of a treasure trove.
Love of worker bees.
All opens to money.

Here still the money tree.

Of a new power.
In a hell.
Of a power that
no hopes may quell.

(Love of work rare
or the more.
Constant care
of the knife.)

       Namesake
of a treasure trove.

6 Coca-Cola

       They taught me too well.

       A zing a ride
a pop in a cup.
Dear art
peals of their laughter
her brittle dish
shallow
     & covered.

They
taught me too well.

7 Heart Song

Your nipple free
is hollow & hard already.

Out of sleep you leap
run from your room in my mind!

Your nipple free
lives it charms of meanness.

Now, lacking art, ahead of me
slight, awful, icy.

Your nipple free ...
(unkind).

Your nipple free ...
(don't cry).

8 Staying

Arch
stasis flying.

Ahead of me swallows the sky.

Ahead of me
swallows the sight of a way.

And I know, arches are reckoned.

Ahead of me.
As the crow flies.

Arch
where the flesh stands.

WHAT YOUR MOUTH IS, FOR INSTANCE

Still, it's good when two or three are foregathered
together and trying to work out what's going on
in the nodding head of a fifth who can't actually speak.
It's something good people do, changed forever
in the encounter. 'He's not really happy, it's part of the mania.'
Neither is he evil or naughty when trying to bite you.
I think of explaining to a clear face, of hypnotism
or snake charming, even that's a superior kind of arm twisting
to real arm-twisting, when the current refuses to fire
along the axon. Your super-glib verbiage won't do
nor will holding the word of God up to ridicule
even if you can't believe in it yourself and simple faith's
an idiot's head swaying to half-remembered hymns.
Turn that radio down, they don't really like it.
Or try wearing an empty dustbin on your head
while others bang on the outside with metal drumsticks.
Somebody with a great wide beam in their eye
is more than likely to be whacking you round the head with it
when they think they're only tossing their own head
in self-righteous annoyance at your spec, their very own
variation on a theme of blaming the afflicted. Is he
responding to stimuli or do we infer inwardness
beyond the non-mysteries of abnormal brain chemistry?
For instance, if benign puts on weight, what happens?
Something we can all bring up at the next meeting
to be addressed by one who can't speak English properly.
Incompatibility of the parental blood groups.
Unsupervised or inexperienced delivery.
Spoon comes mouth goes, spoon goes mouth comes.
And hypertonicity of her muscles in excitement
if a rhesus positive particle should cross over her placenta
we'll be lucky if she's born deformed, or dead,
and circling around these facts of life we'll talk forever –
holding our pieces together, to our own breasts.

IF IF WAS YOUR SON

You'd buy him a box of Maltesers
& hold his trembling hand
drive out with him on a Saturday to Little Holland
& put a big tray of sweets in front of him. If
he could ride a bike ride out with him
to Friday woods
back for a late dinner from the microwave.
Nothing but sadness you say you
just want to know he's being taken care of
if Irene wants everything to go in a straight line
arrange everything in a straight line for her
make her to say please and thank you in Makaton
if she gibbers nonsense run out of the room.
By the sign that reads
                    No Trespassing
kick a soft ball between you for a while
go home, go home
& cook a nice breakfast up
                        there's a nice
girl there
              saving up for the holidays. She will be married
soon, I suppose
                if she's lucky
half a grapefruit for a dowry:
                    a nurse
is a cross on your sleeve
                  a brother is two fists touch
that happens on purpose, accidentally
moving in and out of his bungalow
waiting for his dad to fix it
                     pick up his activity board,
spin his mirror & put the radio on every morning
place a fresh cover sheet on his bed
if necessary
              pay for it out of your pension.

DIARY OF MY TWIN

Nothing to add up to, no fear of you
Your right arm, my letting agent. It's as if
Geraniums grew in an orifice of dark orange trumpets
No building high nought enough,
Roughed up upon the run of the sun's mill of racing fire.
To block in a view
Of where you want to go.
Yes eyes secluded clues of boats, the Seychelles
Listen to it all again, arranged a second
Time might tell this one of
Yellow molars
Last pick stick of shift of viscous black oil
On the bottom of the dipstick
The old wick's turned up high, no longer resting in it.
Denial is my business. Murder is my trump.
Big boulder of a blocked exit
Shaken down a trouser leg, wandered away from it
Watering a home garden with your tears your shit
And turning ever like a severed half
In search of amputated twin. Visitors stories varied, vivid.
Lived livid denial.
Ran away from morphine

Jenny.

Jenny.

Jenny Wren.
Jenny Wrong.

BLACK RAIN

The groaning of a land-boat
is night thoughts a-flowing –

night thoughts a-flowing
sands in an hour-glass
covered by shadows –

covered by shadows
blacker than my words
leaping, unbidden

by the stream that glistens
and passes through –

beneath skies
where the tides murmur
of an opening.

HANDOVER

Under the weather
which is what
                tired means
unable to keep his feet, sat down
pulled up, kept quiet, dazed
eyes ping-ponging. Lifted him
up and into bed, put the cot side
up, snuggles down over his kylie
arms behind his head.
Lights of the snoezelen
might even be cause of fits
glories of Charlotte Church
might be innately religious
lights off, sound off

*

you feel so sorry for the poor little devil
struggling to get up, so pliant to the touch
enraged, knowing you're there
for something

*

travesty

*

A woman snuggles down into the collar
of her pale blue fleece in front of
Emmerdale

Shopping for toiletries, discount

What soap? deodorant? tissues?

Taking the pads out, changing
them from a blue to a green
at night

These are the blah blah of blah

What soap? deodorant? tissues?

*

I've had the fright of my life

*

Jim delivers a big tricycle
from the day centre. I try riding around
the lounge a few times – it's great!
She even goes in reverse, faster
somehow than low-geared forward.

*

13 Ways of Looking at a Nark

*

When

better not struggle too hard
against your negative
                    feelings about it

you'll do yourself a mischief

*

Buy her a clock
to let her know her time's run out

Buy her a hydrotherapy tank
to drown herself in

Buy her a gold locket
full of dust

*

Mother-in-law's Tongue

soak the tongue
wring it out in your ears

IN TOO DEEP

Interest mounting always – a crisp morning
a line borrowed from a song,
to reach within and stare
flinch and stammer, riding out of here
on the opened book of the fields –
a silky stretch of fog,
some lost proverb or word
from the solitary vigil a night keeps.

Asleep tangled in damp linen
dealing out place mats
it will all back up, blistering under your fingers
in the subtle rain, subtle weather,
each error and way alight on a plain slick as milk
where, going home, it's the night staff
in their prudence carry water.

Sleep boat eddies.
Cruel restive groanings & calls
undid the beds
& gall-heaped duvets, spillages
on a shoreline of murmurs –
Empty laughter's their blessing, no hand in mine
the manifold worry that is care
dull memories, spent crimes.

Strike up boldly on your walking frame
the last say has wept out its piece
to slack-jawed barrier faces
learning talk to drown in ink –
To please nay and nay and nobody:
a matchbox, an elastic band,
clothes peg triggers in the palms of my hands
cover up the land with farthings.

The blind were dying to be led,
the play ageing as a play ages.
Answer the phones – a throttle rain,
last of ravaged cornflakes, a spoon.
Night trouble and daily fights:

a sky black with screened icons
& folded underclothes, ironing,
lying in wait for a last madrigal.

It drops towards you on a glider
over the spit-splashed washing,
before the fog ends
after the last flag –
Territory, I believe in you
retching, spitting in fright,
a shallow grave's winter solstice
rising up from the leaky earth.

Slowly they'll march to reach us
who are talking and biting air.
Can a pill hide the gibbous state?
Will a choice feed us?
I slake my thirst, spurning thought
for the swift rotation of a florin.
I parade lies as the ploughing of furrows.
I parade murder as the spring-cleaning of a house.

Let it go. No further reasons
ruthless or broken.
Time's a trouble-healer with a burning coal.
Time's the friend of might, the cessation of play.
Lessons are free to all who flinch –
the prudent will carry water
or listen to me, who suckled
your teats by the fountains of whispering pond

by the coliseum of snore
thoughtfully arranged for the edification of morons.
To look within and stare –
a prayer of half-wits, a prayer of disquiet.
I wanted to trust my mind
a strap-line stolen from a song,
some lost word or proverb
my pocketed spanner, riding out to the fair.

2

PARABLE OF THE HEADLESS WOMAN

All the bits in the garage are out of reach
up in the rafters, waiting to be got down,
pulled out, taken somewhere else, to another,
a trio of Spanish galleons from the auto-jumble
& four spare wheels for the Buick
                              bouncing on their cushions.
Not much remaining here – a generator abolished,
packed in the rented lock up
where the heavier things rest for later redemption.
Files are a rough way of making things smooth.
The ducts, if they overflow, will wash out over me.
Tarps and toolboxes, ambidextrous & professional;
a set of worn-out heartbeats disguised in a rolled up carpet.
No major discoveries here. No
lost snapshots of that solitary Judy you met
(a Blackpool side-show's headless woman)
in the bar of a hotel where you were fitting carpets.
You laughed to hear about her strange job.
She was thinking of giving it up soon.
She smoked a cigarette, shook out her curls.
You'd even been to see her show
a couple of times:
                    she kicked about in a bubbling glass jar,
kept alive by a cluster of plastic tubes at her neck.
Decapitated in a train crash, so it was said
but luckily the next carriage had been full of French surgeons
who patched her up
                    & the strong man lifted two ordinary chairs
at arm's length, one in each hand.
You stepped out of the crowd
                         & tried to lift them both up high,
tumbling, too late: lead weights
                         were attached to each of the legs.

MY NATIVE HOME

I'd read Coleridge's lost novel already
& found a far more careful work
than Biographia Literaria, revealing nonetheless
of an allegorist's underlying plot, of sentences
braided coloured tendons
in an anatomy book
     of Chinese pigtails,
tendrils of a blue smoke across pocked moons:
their craters clearer, closer after reading it
& linked by ten thousand runnels to those others
on the dark side, where starlight poured in
& drove its shuttering engines –
a delicate, a robust machine
the great poet had sketched in early youth
weeping from a lost fight with his brother,
remembering the fairy parlour, skimming flat
stones on the flat Otter. Executed to perfection
each twisted braid wound tight
but on the typescript I examined
each sentence had been upset at a single point
in another slanted hand, for thus, thus
out of kindness, he had suppressed this work
now unfolding in my brain, a slow-worm of
a novel, whose meanings opened & sprang shut
as the powerful electro-magnet it carried
in its long body
    wiped me out.

DOUBTFUL DAYS

Recently I'd come to know more, and my hate
Mostly rearranged itself into the carelessness
Of a brown study in place of that hullabaloo
Which had gained so little through rekindling my appetites.
I'd always known I was one of their number:
Whisperers of rage in breathless thoughts of how
Dreams might tell everything of such recognitions
Such of which no other thought provides exit into the air
Or a sunlight whose fears might still drown you.
My thoughts would be as pairs of loaded dice:
Thrown, thrown again, and taken up once more
Trying to break a run of threes with snake-eyes.
Encirclements of the heart: caring for nothing,
Not even a police helicopter pinpointing my arrest
Or raising up its giant's head to peer at naught.
Until then I had thought only of the interminable days
Of childhood, where in dreams of the perfect drum
I had laboured horizontally over thumb equations
Enacting few of my place duties, never there, at home
But upon the reeling roads, where in my fright
I would make violent entreaties to several floors above
In those blistered and belittling soul-searchings
Which made such a piss-poor show out of my loves.
Back home to dream. To dream in the big dream-bed.
For it was there a prematurely misanthropic son
Built his crocodile promontories out into the dark;
Fished for snapping gods with a night-capped granddad,
A bamboo rod bent in half between the laughing pair
On an ashtray sea leaping with crocs and sharks.

ISABELLE, SA SOEUR

I remember how you came to me in Charleville
on a furlough from your first husband
the architect, the high flier, when I was still
a late student studying Arthur Rimbaud.

I remember the tallest of tall wire-mesh fences
surrounding your father's large, self-built house
as a sort of enclosure around your girlhood
in order to keep the Ardennes' wild boars out.

I remember you dousing your breasts with wine
to make them grow, so that I'd want you
and the stupid list of rules your father sent me
with the timetable of his daughters' bedtimes.

I remember your tallness, your curving spine,
sloping gait; your feet, bigger than mine
so that when I greeted you and we made love
on our feet, it was like facing another man.

You joked that you were no longer a child
while I still was, the roles were reversed,
and you made me another round chocolate cake
in your mother's kitchen, pretending it was for yourself.

I remember so well your unimaginable life,
your incomprehensible letters. I still have them
in a cardboard suitcase, the one I first carried
with a bleached photo of you developed at school.

I remember meeting you again in a supermarket
on Belle Ile, still scruffy, with a sort of nervous arrogance
while your large, boisterous, ill-dressed daughter
demolished a stack of tins in an adjoining aisle.

I remember hearing of your death in a car crash
on your way to work in the mountains near Grenoble,
a psycho-motrice for children. Qu'est ce que c'est, ça?
Carried away by a snowdrift: a small avalanche.

Poor Isabelle, how I still remember you as a girl
in a black cord coat, a cardigan with a floppy collar.
All knees and elbows. A strange girl who wasn't so strange.
Laughing at Harpo in the Maison des Jeunes.

ANTI-HEROES

Imagine that Pope had dedicated himself
to obtaining fair play for hunchbacks,
that, as the most intelligent of their kind
he had tried to represent his tribe
and find a literary analogue for their condition.

Perhaps he could make his verses mis-shapen,
listing, asymmetrical, a bit like himself.
He could make them limp a little, too
and play for sympathy. He didn't though.
He didn't. That's why we've heard of him.

Each crack is at the end of the whip.
And even then they said his satiric bite
was only the bitterness of a cripple.
But I imagine they were probably right.
They are usually, these fountains of opinions.

He certainly asked for their advice on women.
He played the lad in letters. How sitting
between the misses Blount
he had trouble 'to keep myself in my skin',
and they jumped out of theirs in a kind of delicious fright.

How he could place everything in order,
grasshoppers, swine, elephants and men
arranged, arraigned, yet their order's
mocked, turned upside-down, provisional:
a day, a play on which the curtain falls.

Mrs Pope died at Twickenham, still unaware
they say, of the reasons for her son's great fame.
A caterpillar repeats thy mother's grief,
her gardening's undone by its infernal chewing
in an aphorism Blake flung down anywhere.

DANCING ON THE SHIELD OF ACHILLES

I found the busstop at the end of a short, stinking alley
The timetable pinned to a telegraph pole, a driver willing
To take me, refusing my watch in exchange for a ticket.
I am the boy who danced on the shield of Achilles.

I am the boy my father poo-pooed, made me learn poetry
By heart as a punishment for lying, took an erudite neighbour
On my next trip, because he knew the names of heroes.
I am the boy who danced on the shield of Achilles.

I am the boy who received a lecture for his trouble.
I am the boy who got an impatient cuff of the backhand.
I am the boy who rode to the sky on the celestial omnibus.
I am the boy who danced on the shield of Achilles.

I am the boy who thought the authors were characters
And the characters their authors, spinning their wool
Out of their own insides, who was loved for his ignorance.
The daring boy who danced on the shield of Achilles.

Loved for next to nothing, rewarded for being in need
I am the boy who woke up one fine day – and a genius
Told me everything, told me because I knew how to listen.
Because I was the dancing boy on the shield of Achilles.

I am the boy who thought Mrs Gamp most informative
Who thought all and sundry were the best people to tell
Of my discovery, as important as how the babies are made.
I am the dancing, prancing boy on the shield of Achilles.

And I am the man who feels worn out with his telling
By the slights of the mob, the superciliousness of the wise:
They never tire of telling you a dancing boy is nothing
Compared to a hero who turns his shield up to the skies.

OVER THE ROOFS

Yesterday evening I walked out, as usual, in search of a little poetry,
not enough to tire me completely: a small poetry that would impart to
      my limbs
that loose feeling we get after a bicycle ride or a light workout.
Poetry that hangs here like a mist above the sloping rooftops
whose silk rags sometimes float down to one when the sun is setting,
a poetry that is everywhere, over the roofs of those little workshops
      above the town.
I wanted to be their best friend; instead I am the stalker of these things
and I tell myself that what has little value for the people
may justifiably be appropriated by any wanderer hereabouts
as a button-hole or a casually picked nosegay one places in the band of
      one's hat.
Yesterday evening, bored by the closing market
I climbed Rue Jean-Jacques to where the commercial quarter
begins to peter out into a number of smaller premises.
I am telling you this, but there is a danger you'll laugh at me
as though I had come home with a pair of unmatched shoes
or some curious vegetable that reminded me of your childhood
would be better, in that land of departed shadows – you know.
I never slow down there, simply walk past, leaning forward a little.
Lights are on inside and sometimes a radio is playing
hits of the day, muffled by the metal workshop doors,
painted green, I have noticed, as I have noticed much up there
floating over the corrugated roofs, the wisps of it floating
down to where I am searching for the poetry of workshops
      high above the town.

Yesterday I made my usual journey. But to my surprise
the mechanics had all lined up to greet me. At first I was afraid
but they were not unfriendly, merely curious, like me. Hey,
one of them called, Hey you there. Do you live at the top of this hill?
Because I do, and I've never seen you there. Leave her,
leave her be, said by an older man, who reminded me
of your great comedian, Oliver Hardy. No, I said, no.
I am only walking for a while. I like the sound of your working
there, it reminds me of something I have yet to discover.
I'll help you, said the younger man. His companion laughed
shyly, incorrigibly. He had funny spots and I wanted to hug him.

You will discover much that way, replied their comedian father.
I looked past their shoulders into a workshop's interior.
And I laughed at them and them at me, and I pulled on up
to the top of the hill to where the whitewashed houses
were closing up their shutters, surrounded by low cement walls
gardens planted with red geraniums and bicycle handlebars –
respectable homes of the men in their dirty workshops
and empty washing lines: these too had a special poetry.

MARIANNE MOORE GOES TO SEE THE FARMER

What else could one possibly go to see a farmer about but a pig,
a white porcelain pig he has kept in his window, and seeing
that a sale of his belongings – farm tools, livestock, and so on –
was about to be held, I thought I'd make a bid: a few shillings
and the pig I'd admired so when buying his mustard-grain sausages
would be mine. I wondered what I would find to do with it.
The sale took only a couple of hours; it all went, and very quickly.
But afterwards I saw that the porcelain pig had not been sold.
I offered him five pounds. No, he said, you can have him for nothing.
I thanked him. I will stand him on my desk, I said, to remind me
of all the delicious sausages I have eaten. He's too pale, said the farmer,
an albino. I never knew why he had that sly smile on his face.
It is because he knows he would be indigestible, I replied. Yes.
Yes. I will put him in the hallway, to guard my visitors' umbrellas.

THE UNTELEPORTED MAN

Corridors full of a strange tumbleweed, glutinous stuff
that blew in after the security accident on Arcturus Six.
The culprit for that one definitely the idiot Malackian.
He's safe now, bastard, telling lies about it at Proxima Base
while I am alone in this tattered floating cavern of hides,
its skins loose and torn, letting the black starlight in.

Each day I wash my face and I shave in very hot water
and gorge myself on the canned sardines I found here.
I'm getting fat on this diet, which must be an irony.
Because this is definitely the very last scroll of the story
beginning one day five years ago in high optimism
when all of us were new graduates from Psi-academy.

Something growing over the surface of my eyeballs.
The walls of the ship, my sleeping bag, everything
has taken on a subterranean greenish glow. I don't know.
I don't remember much about it any longer, I look
out at an approaching meteor shower, I eat my sardines
and I try hard to let what passes for my mind go.

It's not difficult, not if you're me, my tools fused
somewhere in the last days of the drawing of food-straws.
It was a strictly done thing, leaving everyone their dignity.
You can't fault the training – its there when it counts.
I turned out to be the last unteleported man, the last
unteleported woman, Irina, jumped three days ago.

I've been talking to one of the little garbage carts.
Released from their gladiatorial function they've formed
a steering committee for garbage cart rights. They say
it doesn't matter that there's no-one here to stop them.
For as long as it lasts isn't a real concept to them.
Still, you've got to admire their sheer bastard persistency.

I'm glad I haven't got any old flicks or photographs.
Instead I tried to get them to let me join in their debates.
They discussed it fully, and the chief little garbage cart
who apparently has a final casting vote, said no dice.

I suppose I was hurt, but fair enough. I'm obviously
not one of them, or of anybody or of anything, I guess.

Our mission was noble if you avoided attachments
But I can't truthfully say I succeeded in that respect.
Perhaps a certain type of person is attracted to the service.
The do-gooding kind who battens on to the creatures
due to a lack of identity with our own sad species.
Jesus, if I eat any more of these sardines, I'll explode.

Much of what we have taken for thought is merely kipple;
a glutinous, mutinous tumbleweed building up in deep snow-drifts.
But I know Irina will remember me, in her terms, forever
and I respected her decision to dance amongst the stars.
I can still hear her calling out to me across the great ether
in a prearranged homing signal: "Ulula-ulula-ulalalalume."

ONE FOOT IN THE GRAVY

There was an interesting lull in the conversation
occurring towards the bottom of the third bottle of claret
as Trevor began to speak to us of his childhood,
not in the usual way of anecdotes of deprivation
but in that glowing manner only wine produces,
the blush of the grape which makes us shameless
in our myth-making, and utterly convinced of our truths.

His were to do with the goodness of his people. There
were his own struggles to achieve, of course, the obstacles
placed in his path, obstacles he had surmounted,
but, of all things, the innocence of his younger brother
particularly an inability to conceive of the evils of the world
as anything other than the actions of a few bad men
who had somehow managed to hoodwink all the others.

I resigned myself to listening to floods of sentiment
thinking of the mechanics of Conrad, soldiers in Kipling
and of how the populist delusions of these great writers
had rendered these passages almost unreadable to us
the beneficiaries of hindsight and of higher education.
Trevor continued his presentation of stupidity as a virtue.
By this time we were all asleep with our eyes open.

I wondered idly if our employer's sad insistences
were merely a cover-up for cruelties he'd experienced
in childhood, cruelties he later meted out to others,
or the product of guilt at his own superior abilities:
a result of some genetic quirk or other, no doubt
which had carried him to where one must deal with evil
on a daily basis, where it is safest to assume the worst.

I said nothing of all this, naturally, and busied myself
with the adroit removal of another cork. My colleagues
nodded puppyish agreement. Although it would be unfair
to say they were simply yes-men, Trevor had effectively
undermined the common basis of our convivial talk.
Eventually he ran down. Meanwhile we had to sit there
a row of drunken dummies: uneasy, silent, a little afraid.

LOGGING ON/GIMME THE LIGHT

Looking out of the window at the side of some building
flat language riming the kerbs with snow
whereas even bare trees over school wall . . .
Billet Road less than snug with its blue plaque on a council house
on the site of Monoux's house, William Morris's museum
I suggest might be a place to go if you were depressed
alone and wanted to look at something beautiful
beyond all this, behind my back the year ten girls
work on their synchronised routine, the past,
the part where you turn round and show them your erase –
pulling up in time to straighten an elephant tie
buckle my belt tighter over the mound of clay.
They showed me their club dance.
Tanisha can do an old lady on a stick, that was yesterday
a witty child with her body, otherwise just cool
cooler than me by a long skidding chalk
peering up through her beads in the canteen, stoned love.
I could be such a hit if it wasn't for the spoilsports:
myself on the bus, climbing into everyone's skin
lurching through the musical chairs, plotting their moves
in search of a contract high. Did you enjoy that, sir?
Who's the best dancer? I am. I am.

ZENITH

He knew he had reached the top when he saw Zenith.
She was a sensible girl who paid him no attention
bending her head low over a page full of her writing.
All of his life he had been looking for a true opinion
but when he saw her he knew there was no option.
Zenith, her name was the highest point he could imagine
right there at the nadir of his life's expectations.

How could he make her look up from her book of days
in which she was studying lineaments of her future
as he had once studied the limbs of a fresh young tree
to see where it grew up out of the ground and into blue sky?
In such a beautiful country, whose waters replenished,
there could be no mistake, no possibility of a lie.
And the name of that country was to be called Zenith.

Her parents had named her after something high
but she would far rather have had an ordinary name.
From time to time she looked up and watched birds go by
on their way south, because it was the end of summer.
After a time her friend Damilola came along the path
to sit beside her; after a time she got up, continued
along that path to the palace of earthly wisdom.

In a country where there was nothing to do but aspire
nothing could disturb the meditations of Zenith —
her brain was more powerful than a powerful computer.
She looked out through her eyes at the page she read
and wrote at the same time with her eyes of blazing fire.
And so he walked past her, an angry, shuffling man
who knew one thing only: he had seen Zenith.

She closed her book of days in time to go home for dinner
on a bus that would be stopping at the edge of the park
carrying her safely home through the gathering dark
in that city of shadows where the men knew nothing.
And she looked out at the blur of its swift passing.
Even then that man was inclined to think she was only an idea.
But she wasn't. Zenith was at the top of everything.

MARTHA AND MARY

Whenever you meet two girls, one of them will believe
and one will be sceptical; the name of the credulous girl
is always Mary; the sceptical one will be called Martha
running your barcodes over her reader with half an eye
on the queue, on some undecided loiterer at the back
who might, at last moment, opt for her dreamy-eyed sister.

Martha has a new haircut, a cap of darkness streaked
with purple highlights. Under it she has a face like heaven,
a black cup tipped to drink all the light in a supermarket
and reflect it, reflecting bad things back where they come
from an awkward customer who thinks of nothing; she
gets up, cools off, slams the empty baskets on a stack.

Mary is still washing the Lord's feet, raptly listening
to a new parable suggested to him by her act of devotion.
Martha thinks that a stone rolled over Lazarus's tomb
would be better left in place. He is dead, already rotting.
And the Lord countermands her, and he will be right
this time as the last; Martha must be happy to be wrong.
Mary claps her hands: I always knew, I always knew.

But Martha is never glum for long. She finds things
generally where she left them, ready to pick up the pieces
of her sister's broken life, last time she was taken in
by a man who had nothing but honourable intentions,
of a sandal nobody else was going to finish mending.
Something will have to do its turn, its second turn.
And Martha is the person who will make this happen.

Mary is pitied and desired, always one last temptation
to be redeemed, of course, in a reserved place in heaven
for listening to the truths of her true, wayward heart;
doing the right-wrong thing, being rescued sometimes
as her eyes shine with conviction, ready for sacrifice,
to offer her comfort where none is possible or needed.
Beautiful she is; and loyal too; and sensible she isn't.

Martha has no real parable of her own, except this one.
The parable is of her beauty alone, her torch of darkness
to light you into the dank underworld of your own tomb.
Don't expect to find her warmth there, just your change,
the momentary touch of her hand. And if you insist on
thanking her, she will only smile at you. "You're welcome."

BOYS FROM THE SOUTH COUNTRY

It started when we buried granddad in the backyard
and convened an annual reunion to worship his bones
later the beginnings of a clan structure emerged
whether by melding or subdivision is anyone's guess.
Mine is that the South was in my veins, calling, calling
it's better down here, so polish up your vowels
and get your dad's leather jacket out of mothballs
and don't bother shaving, they like it rough
on the way home from a house party in Moss-side
light of the yellow sodium lamps
catching at motes of drifting asbestos, fondling
all you ever hoped of love or children or men
of the poetry crowd. Get back to where you don't belong.

The first time ever I saw your face I thought the sun
and the moon and the stars played the chords
haltingly at first, but growing in a confidence trick
I hoped to catch off you like a dose of one-hand clapping
which you solved by turning to your neighbour:
Spud me. Spud me. Spud me. They do that thing everywhere
by shithouse walls, blood-fluke in the brain of an ant
determining your only son's delusions of grandeur.
So kill me with your song. OK, here's where I take over.
Because I can, you know, and if you can you do
never you mind a politicians' pocketful of soap-on-a-rope
a clan sprawling and brawling out of Hampton Wick.
Announcements better unmade, like beds, like this one
that rolling and tumbling ain't done me no harm.

I fell in love with a boy from the North country long ago
and so did everyone else. I kept his address
in a locket near my heart, wept in the supermarket
for the things you couldn't buy there, helplessly watching
as old left celebs assembled their frugal breakfasts of champs.
Go get 'em, Tariq. And tell 'em all that Tiny says hello.
He slid under the ropes, lived to fight another day
I guess, remaining to this of approximately the same height.
Reach up and fetch him down a packet of fresh Spinach.
Muswell Hill. The winds hit heavy on the borderline.
It's grim down south, mounds of flowers on the pavement

commemorate some poor little sod everyone loved
caught against the glass at the wrong angle in the wrong fight
replenished for weeks by his bruvs and bros
by the cashpoint a signed twelve inch by Nelly Furtado.

You miserable bastard, Dylan. I'm not going to send you my book.
I think our suffering is just more grist to your plot-mill.
I know what a broke down engine is, and you're not one
lengthing out more of your stuff from Echo's cotton reel
your chicken neck, the only twitching nose left in the pantheon.
Your works will outlive mine, they have already.
Because of your mercury mouth and your language of napoleons.
Because of my poor words I spit out in my hand like hen's teeth
neither rare nor precious, like my clan, my laughing stock,
my laughing gear wrapped around a ham sandwich
my ancestors stepping up to the no more auction block
where indentured sycophants bought us under the hammer.

Now and then there's a fool in the sweet rye.
It started when we buried granddad in the backyard
and old Walter, Walt Kilfoyle, took off his pork-pie hat
and started to dig the foundations of a cottage he had long fancied building
in the heavy, sticky clay of the London bog-country
big enough for a family of two adults, eleven children.
And it started with the myth of this first original day.
And it started by us repeating a one simple story
to drown out the neighbours' risible counter-myths
speaking of their own fantastic beings in far, impossible countries.

I was Queen Victoria's footman, Henry
at the foot of the 1861 census
an afterthought lingering as a half-credited ghost;
Middlesex, East Mollesey aged 24 years, born in about 1837
immediately forgotten by a whole parish of Kilfoyles
despite a great-niece who cleaned the grace-and-favour apartments
at Cardinal Wolsey's briefly-owned Hampton Court Palace,
like Walt's an altogether too desirable residence
to stay in one family, Henry I's not Henry VIII's
who got his Hampton Court while chewing the Tudor fat
premier Elvis impersonator of his day, holding his gut in for the pictures:

a career coasting along for centuries on one measly hit —
probably ghost-written by his cheeky footman
the day before he inspected his own patent shoes
from the tumbril. I know so many stories like that.
My own fabrications are as good as yours, sir
as a musket-ball will outrun even a scalded kitchen cat
unwilling to dedicate his gut to a game of Real Tennis
while the Queen had never spoken of me by name
except once in a fit of pique at the empty jar of tincture of cannabis.
They fled from me whom sometime did me bed
& the four posters offered a reward for my head.
What might have been a family triumph ended in disgrace.

In this place certain men must hide their face:
the whole mess is crowned with its laurel of doubt,
unwarranted, unwarrantable difficulties
bedog our footsteps with deep, irregular begorrahs,
a misrecognised personal eccentricity
acclaimed as the accomplishment of the ages
and the slip of a rocking-horse winner reneged on
by the inhabitants of blind, closing up windows.
Alone with a sixpenny paper in some empty, over-lit Araby,
a dream in your heart, a dream in your black heart,
you're pulled towards a cavernous false-ceiling
vaulted with crows' feet enclosing dirty panes
when outside night falls upon mean little streets
that will never hurl themselves upon the great:
a maze fit only for a drunken, stupid king.

All of it had to be true, like poetry
tested on the rump, a good stick
makes you say ouch whether you would or no.
These repeated acts of definition
are acclamatory by definition, true chips
are gold chips on your shoulders, I mean
epaulettes of ivory coast doubloons —
a tune played on the silver spoons
goes clack clacketty clack but oh my soul is pure
my heart pure beating meat fit for a lineage of kings and queens
the founders of the great cities of gold.

Now you can learn to count the days till I return
as the great leader, the great father of men
and of women, for a bright aura of healing dances around my head
purplish for I have loved, I will love again
because even the dogs like me, according to their dubious owners
when they sit close to my leg, a Tower of Babel,
listening to the massive circulation of my blood
speaking to them of known things.

The first time ever I saw your face, I thought the sun
and the stars were shining like cities
to be scraped off, losing chips, by the croupier of an idiot-board.
The first ever I saw your face I thought fun
flirtation, fucking, I thought of the moon
starring in my own double feature alongside your body
blood-fluke in the pants of an ant, a stinger
in the picnic-basket filled with love-hearts
which fizzed away in a tumbler of star-black bible gin.
I decided to apologise for nothing, nothing
last time ever I saw your face, my last grin
was sucked up by the spare MacDonalds' straw
you carried for camel's backs & the souls of men.
Beyond a joke, a yolk I have never stopped
dipping my little red soldier in, loving you is
like that, like loving another with murder in my heart
so I will never be expecting you to call me
or answering my own questions for you, it's
no more than the way it all is, dear friend.

Waylaid by passing strangers, a myth of the weather peeling off
strips of bacon to bracket a soon to be cooked egg,
halving a tomato for the red eyes to clear a fried slice under your belt
to sow marble-chip stars in the fresh black pour of the tarmac
until another immigrant's front drive can be seen from the ionosphere.
Sticking a roof on the world before it ends on Friday the Thirteenth
and making sure the bloody cheque has three days to clear.
Removing the stump of an ancient tree that grew from a planted spear
so they say at the pump, sparkling on your back like cold electricity.
Wee Gerrard's bunked off school is looking for a good slap.
Walt Kilfoyle coasts by on his old black bike, no brakes, no brake-rods,

a brick-filled hod on his back and a future in the lap of the gods.
Advice about women is cheaper than women, that's for sure, boy.

Will it really do to keep maundering on like this
Janus-faced, like the history of any institution
redrawn, renamed with the old names so many times
until a withered tree stump has become the basis of representation,
the phyles refilled from each other until genos is
transmuted to ethnos, a process close to alchemy
offering to clear its false-trail through nameless mud
when mix-up matrimony may not only be preferable
but is what happened anyway, a true equality
a tune circulating for millennia, popping out here
and there. There is no answer to that, musicians
play on and don't spare the painted charioteers
flaking off of some dim frieze. Dear Berrigan, he died.
It happened – love, marriage, children – everything.

Poetry and myth continued to flourish
in the dark ages of my construction
for the works of Samuel Beckett and William Burroughs
were achieving considerable circulation.
I decided to begin recording the tape of my future life
because I had no past to speak of or cut to ribbons.
Spoiled by an early success, I gave it up for lent
only to discover I'd seen all of it coming
and fell to celebrating myself backwards
as the source of what I had discovered
in my world's cultural productions. A hammer fell.
Travelling clocks snapped shut like vanity cases.
I slipped one in my back pocket and left my parents flat
remembering them on the road for comfort
until the tenth woman I met smiled at me
and took me to a house of many hanging shawls
where they lived on a broth of nougat & rice, al dente
stuck between their teeth. I watched hers rotting.
And that's when I began to tell her of my crazy dreams
believing myself when I caught her dark eyes.

THE CLOWNS

The clowns gathered at night on the same spot, under lights
provided for other purposes, by a municipality indifferent
to their existence, or mine, practising their old routines
and passing a hat amongst themselves; there were no passersby
in that quarter – which could mean slim pickings for a clown.
They weren't always the most generous of audiences for
their own comrades' antics, knowing as they did all the tricks
of what had been their trade, before human laughter died out,
an eventuality few could have predicted, I mean humanity
growing sombre to the point of being totally po-faced
about its own predicament, or what was even less predictable
less cruel in its assessment of the likely sufferings of others;
not other races, of course, but members of our own breed
upon whom misfortune had smiled, or perhaps frowned
leaving little to do for the legions of unemployed clowns.

Anyway, there were near-nightly gatherings of these unpopular beings
who far from being disconsolate amongst themselves had created
a little island of merriment, of continued laughter. They'd no spare change
for one another, but did provide the other clowns with an astringent
yet supportive audience, as though it were a matter of duty in their eyes
to keep laughter alive, helped out in this noble endeavour by the fact
that many of them were buoyant, naturally optimistic people, although
there were always the darker clowns, for whom a rush of any sort
was generally a rush of foreboding, a talent that at last proved useful
in the last days, when humanity needed to be warned, in a light way,
that any future excuses for celebration were likely to be few and far
between during coming months, and where they did occur were likely
to call for something oblique: something slyly suggestive of pique.

The clowns are less important in this story than whatever took
the spring out of the step of humanity. It could have been many things:
a war, an unstoppable pestilence slaying a generation of children, an
alien invasion or the sudden triumph of some miracle-working dictator
such as the socialist pub bore envisaged by H.G. Wells, The Man
Who Could Work Miracles – abolishing night and day in his futile bid
for a perfect world. But it was mainly the persistent clowns who continued
to intrigue me. Not that I ever used to pay attention to their antics
except with a kind of sinking feeling that meant, for me, failure

to wall out an all too common sense of people being comical
rather than tragical, as they are when struck by lightning, or can be;
for, like the Wells character, The Man Who Could Work Miracles,
I had used to take myself and my many opinions far too seriously.

There were even those who said that I was worse than the others
and that would at least suggest a reason why I felt I must atone
by sneaking over to where the clowns congregated in their car park,
making myself invisible in shadows, taking care not to laugh.
Or perhaps I had only found a way to continue being myself,
that is, out of step. The clowns generally rehearsed the same trick.
I think it involved a bowler hat, a scoop of inverted darkness
out of which something miraculous was always about to appear.
There were the usual delays, the business, mugging to a crowd
which had begun to disperse before some of these young fellows
were born, and the young women who had latterly come
to take up the lost art of clowning, may have been equally in the dark
as to the meaning and origins of mirth in our people's history.
And the bowler hat with its glow of promise – of redemption?
a pound of butter? – may have had a different meaning for these girls,
the last generation of our clowns; I hope they didn't know it.
For their ignorance may yet rekindle the lost spirit of merriment.

NATHANIEL HAWTHORNE

Two men are fruitlessly waiting for the arrival of another.
After a time one of them decides to hang himself.
Just one of many stories you decided not to write, Nathaniel
Hawthorne, lover of foreign travel, where romance grows out of a ruin
and the face of the man who hides himself from question
is that of a murderer whose vanity eats the lives of others
who hires a handmaiden of death to do the honours.

Nathaniel Hawthorne is silent at the table of honour
where he has just met Herman Melville, whom he admires.
They had corresponded about the tyranny of the democratic public.
There is little to say, apparently. Both sit sipping claret
at the end of a great struggle to end up in the middle of nowhere.
The two cleverest monkeys in the United States of America.
The authors of Moby Dick and the Scarlet Letter.

Nothing is going on in this story except the waiting.
Nothing is happening except the deferment of your pleasure.
Nothing is going to be revealed about the meaning of myth.
Nothing is implied by a comparison of matches.
Nothing is journeying in the end to meet its shoemaker.
Nothing is slipping and sliding, rolling and tumbling.
Nothing is certain. Nothing is going to curb America.

THE VICTORS

. . . But it was impossible to save the Great Republic.
The multitudes were prostrate before Popoatahualpacatapetl
whose Viceroys continued to hold mastership by his name.
Little Johnny Microbe and his loyal band of sisters and brothers
had completely failed to break out of their respective places in the food chain.
Indeed, they had got no further than to blame the Great Spirit
for not existing, not even that far, since their lamenting cries
consisted entirely of a long series of bitter exclamations
that what had been given to them once had been taken away
by His cruelty alone, who bit out their heart with grief only
to offer it to others as nourishment, a sort of juicy meal,
which they, dying from starvation, had little choice but to accept.

The Outlines of History (Suppressed) was now taught in secondary schools
perhaps not a text for those who would fail to graduate in woodwork
but looked forward to eagerly by those deemed fit for Truth
or that version of it propounded by the loins of Popoatahualpacatapetl
who thought such cries of despair at the inevitability of his coming
rather suitable for the instruction of youth, inevitability being, like hindsight,
easier to accept with a meal of the forequarters of Phoebe Gray Spider
than a lot of irritating what ifs and the joining together of retracted paws.
And wasn't there something rhetorical, and therefore dubious about
sentimental anthropomorphism, if only that it was sentimentally
                                                    anthropomorphic?
Better by far to join your teeth together in the person of Little Dora Sparrow
she whose mamma harpooned Sammy Pinch-Bug with her beak.

Jimmy Crown-of-the-Creation you may be, they seemed to be saying,
but even so you are not "The Prodigy" told of in those old books we
gave you of the days when army after army, sovereignty after sovereignty, went
down under the mighty tread of the shoemaker. Popoatahualpacatapetl,
                                                    buyer and
seller of nations, of dark peoples, labour power and characteristic songs.
White people, new buckra come, one, two, tree, all de same! He be die,
                                                    he be sick!
In my bitterness I had forgotten the quick step of your pink heel into my room.
You seemed to know everything and nothing of the bad people, me.
But there's nothing to be done about it except moveable type and New Hampshire
rolling away from it all like old Hampshire, like the waves of the sea
onto which you have paddled with your cargo of fruit, my brown sisters.

The Great Republic has released its cargo of "love bombs" over targets
chosen by Popoatahaulpacatapetl himself, who comes now and then
in a great vision we had been awaiting for so long, sleeping through all

                                                  our days
as his gnat armies swept to victory over far off lands; swift shadows
stealing all that the departed Great Spirit had left for the use of everyone . . .
until even our placards shone with the faces of victorious enemies . . .
unless . . . unless . . . brothers and sisters may hold one another strongly
and weapons of thought be vanquished by our turbulent dreams, by our arms.

I'm telling you this story with a straight face; it's to make you laugh
not because I expected you to take my jumping frogs so seriously
like some fools do, because they have placed a bet on the outcome,
but because I loved how you sang it out loud, insistent in your defiance
and, although ignorant of the deleted passages in blind books,
processing new information in your own way, adding to stocks of experience
you fitted so easily to those old tunes picked up from the radio
as light and necessary as air, a cloth to protect the nape of your neck.
Allegro passages in my fables; in your life my helping hands.

TALKING WITH THE DARK HORSE ABOUT HIS MONEY

It wasn't that you had betrayed me
More a sort of suspicion that you were about to
Go the way of all flesh, through the oaken door
I had arranged to be left open, flapping in the brisk weather
That I knew would be irresistible to you, even
Inviting a comment, or was it a passing comet

Streaking across the sky with your name on
Or mine, as graffiti by some greater poet
To be erased by the air-stream, or was it the gulf stream?
Anyway, a warm wash before they hung you out to dry
On the Maginot line between two armies –
A thin red line is paper thin but paper is generally white.

I remember thinking of your attitudes
Not much but a little, the attitudes of a spoilt rich child
Who hasn't yet been completely ruined.
That task was to be my own although I failed to complete it
Before the gong sounded and a war was slated to begin.
Does this begin to sound in any way familiar?

If so, I apologise, though not as sorry
As I will be, eventually, after all the portents are gathered
And counted like votes cast against me
By casual agency of the other runners
Whose insistent hoofs and rumps at the trough
I'd thought were there merely to flank me for a short ride.

By the time your blood's up it's all over
And you are again cleaning out the Augean stables
With a toothbrush on a long piece of wire.
Fiery and Snuffy just left for the last rodeo in Montana
Throwing the Houlihan in your regretted absence.
In the recurring dream I was Cinderella.

By the way, did I ever tell you the one about
That blind man who wrecked W.C. Fields' general store
With a slender white cane and a repeated demand
For Kumquats? No? I believe his little dog helped a lot
Wheeling and barking that way, whilst W. C. Fields
Implored him to desist. No way, man. It's A Gift.

I used to think you actually had it, although ignorance
Would have served as well at the heaped counter
Where what you wanted was never really for sale.
A blind man's blind insistency is almost heroic,
As is his destructiveness, although not for himself
Nor us, for whom he is just another gem-like comic character.

I know it's difficult to tell what's properly yours
Once you've rubbed shoulders with half the world.
In your case a forgetful laugh seems to suffice
As, chewing the pen, a dimple spreads fetchingly
Down the dead centre of your wide forehead
And words just spring out from nowhere, it's like "Eureka!"

We're at the half way mark now. The maiden fillies
Showing their mettle, or is it fettle, against the fence.
The bay is a squeezin' though a gap, it's the tiny eye
Of a needle, while a bobtail nag has this fool's gold
Riding on her illustrious, beribboned pom-pom.
Dem days gone forever, way down the Swanny river.

I remember Lapp dancing involved herds of reindeer.
You plotted their migratory routes across pack ice.
Dancing started when you put up your house of sticks
In a force ten gale, and the famous white powder
Cleaned out your sinuses, your poor synapses
Jumping with white sparks like iced up switching gear.

Spewing their envious bile, they've shuffled off
To country retreats, to wander Sunday bug-eyed
Inspecting empty pavements for interlopers' fleas.
Dog flecks can hop in from just about anywhere.
Herodotus was a dopus compared to Pope and Homer.
Plato's shadows of ideas? He was suffering from mild glaucoma.

What made Jude so *gullible?* Haw haw haw.
Always the injured party animal, a beleaguered snoop
Huffing into the safe berth of a picked off scab –
Preferably someone else's. I suspect my juice is juicier.
And if they keep it raw and open long enough
I'll even thank you for it with another free poem

As you adumbrate my miserable rage. Ah me!
How everyone wants to get into your pants!
And that's not the worst of it. None of us is immune
To perverse emotions attendant on a bit of flattery
After all, I'm longer in the tooth than any prehistoric tiger
Who might have trouble getting into his own.

I'm afraid none of my holy illusions is intact.
Although I'm not quite yet a toy of the weather
Pestilence has caught me round the gut and chops.
Still, I'd rather do my own nit-picking, thank you:
A kind of make-weight candidate on a closed short list.
I'm not auditioning as the fourth musketeer.

It might be sophisticated of me to move in
On you, as the pastel girth of another good day
Turns into something not even worth a memory
At least, not as I'd have it, the boys flopping off the logs
While kind elderly helpers nodded, passing
You their tightly furled diploma, a baton

Cut from a new broomstick, the good witch
Offering you her free flying lessons around the quad
When it is your own questionable reserves of puff
That will prove to be crucial on the day
As you mount a slight incline to find a young God
Picking his toenails with your lost implement.

And, if I may finally be permitted to say a few
Words on my own behalf, hopefully opening
Another book on my own remaining life span:
For the forgotten child you have robbed me of so cruelly
Wandering on foot in the great dark woods
Where bad men live, hidden by daylight, looking for me.

EVERYTHING THAT HAS HAPPENED

Let me say what I wanted to say in the way I meant it
When I tried to write one of your poems under canvas
Her body perspiring beside me, an opening flower
Distraction of the heaving sea, rocks strewn in the fields
A badger padding by on the way to the inn of our happiness
O let the coins pay for our dark beer there
A road turning at the corner of the tumbled mountain
A stream she waded sharp and cold in a cotton dress
Lifted at the hem of the world
A strange milestone I planted like a gypsy
Owls hooting their bitter omens of our forbidden love.

Let me say what I wanted to say the way I meant it
I might have saved the day, pressed a flower in my book
On the train I met a strange young monk
Whose father had given him everything for the journey
Only my kindness was necessary, my poor kindness
Wasted on strangers and those with something to give up
A star in the sky shining down on me, balefully
Youth spooling out, and returning, a moebius strip
Arriving at the point of departure some years later
Unable to join us on the night ferry
Losing my time on the wild coast of her girlhood –
Let somebody say what happened to him. Let me say
What I wanted to say in the way that I meant it.

JAMES HANLEY, PROLETARIAN NOVELIST

Into the furnace of their days, their spent nights choking
In the slack shovelled onto hot ashes
Left over by a knocked-off shift;
The second mate's brother-in-law
Getting away with murder, cruel jokes, a carelessness
Because it's only John Reilly on his last trip.
John Reilly, thin as a rake, a horse comb of broken teeth.
Let's give the stupid old bastard some gyp.
They're feeding the flames of a justified self-contempt.

Anger boils his protruding bones in squid ink.
Bitten off articles are more than he can chew in the bunk
Woken up by slops from the sky –
The parting gift of some minor stand-in of God.
Sure, didn't Duffy speak up for him?
Not too loud, not too loud, for wasn't he next for the chop?
John Reilly, dreaming of his children's births
At the end of a twisted, worn out rope of life.
Hanley crawls down a dark tunnel for eighteen months
Back to squeeze another cup of juice out of them
Into the cold furnace of their days, their nights
For a limited edition, unlimited pains.

John Reilly is a stander of drinks, of rounds.
And a meeter and greeter of the cruellest jibes with a face of flint
Folded out of paper, an origami proletarian
Smelling of the lamp, of lamp-black
Of stokers black enough for Nancy Cunard's feather bed.
And a dropper of pennies into poor men's boxes.
All except for the tired horses.
All except for the tired horses.
Who don't get anything at all, not from him.
Not a drink of water, not a bale of hay.

A dark pint and a lemon dash –
A man gets the same pie in his face ten times in a row in a day
And we laugh on with and at him in respite
From our own failure to ring the bell,
Complacent as ever in our boozy sacrifice.

Don Quixote drowned amongst the windmills
Of that history, their bright sails are full of a white sand
And turning, turning slowly – but it's only
Dry bones being ground to fine flour
To dab on the face of a pantaloon.
He stands at the furnace that has eaten away his body.
He is standing, really, between two hells.
Standing there without fear or the hope of justice.
John Reilly! His heart is beating quickly.
The cry of his name goes up: John Reilly! John Reilly!

Or he is like Mr Dunford, the captain of troop ship A.10
In that turbid, harrowing novel, Hollow Sea,
Delivering up his cargo of stinking corpses
To the doorstep of the British Admiralty.
Dumping the consequences of their wrong orders
At their lily-white feet. An accuser of false authorities
Who knows there is no justice. None, not really.

And it is not a single tragedy he writes of
But degradation, of generation after generation
Folding into one another. Getting another one, sucking tripes
For a treat, taking their problems to a fortune-teller
Who lives on their hopes, their vain hopes
Soon forgotten – except he doesn't forget.
He is their rememberer. Writing, in that case, for nobody.

Broken water, splintered truths
Are offered finally to an old woman in the sky.
Her letters posted nowhere – to a dead son
Invented, thought of at the end of a broken evening –
A broken mind, dancing on waves.

IN THE BRITISH MUSEUM

The Assyrians carved every single fish in the Tigris
counting heads on its muddy banks while the nimble charioteers
rode down their fleeing enemies, the humans; leaning back,
their claw fingers close around one last rock, handily, magically
to hand as a centaur's spear is about to pierce their hides
really this time, the long struggle expressed in juxtaposed
diagonals having resolved itself at last into unexpected victory
in a passage chiselled off by a later chiseller, a jewelled
monosyllable rising to the lips of today's slain. Arghh!
And we're heading off into the queue for the cafeteria
then, onto the benches, moody heifers lowing at the price
of an organic cappuccino grown in volcanic soil, try it.

In his film *The Rebel*, Tony Hancock demands a coffee without froth
and wonders over it if his sculpture of Aphrodite at the Waterhole
will ever be rescued. It's fallen down through his landlady's floorboards.
Will it be embedded permanently there in Irene Handl's front room
for the future instruction of the lower middle classes? They'll
never learn, while we enjoy spoiled fruits, as contradictorily
voluptuous as a stolen bar of white chocolate, a latter day Milky Bar.
Waiting for the kid to ride. Being clever at everyone else's expense.
But it's true, Chris. Most artists in the world are mere carvers of fish,
deep waves resembling a bed of chips on a finely shredded lettuce,
perhaps intricate painstaking works, even incompetent ones surviving,
saying serve yourself, there's as much of this as you can eat.

A lion's head in the desert and Persephone's pert little breasts.
Her mum, Demeter, crying into the river, blighting our crops
& offering seasonal return by way of a sop. The Gods couldn't
give a shit, they're dead drunk at the helm. As the Greeks so wittily
observed – if it really was wit rather than a cynical celebration.
We're bogged in the nay-saying cult of the losers. Woe to them!
Better to use the strength of Mars to slay the bull of Marathon!
Because the press will say whatever it likes. Because glucose
makes you comatose after the first rush of happiness and Scooby
says if you're stuck in the firing line, history is one long "Yikes!"

Waiting for microwave pings of millennia, the white cod fish
a same old white block frozen solid in the middle, drifting back

to your own life, the usual small reasons for your unhappiness
presenting themselves with the regularity of stolen snacks
in never settled routines – you couldn't wish them away if you tried.
I'm packing up to move tonight at six: Still following the van.
I'm expecting things of the world – a bad mistake, the world.
Friendly fire clipped my wings. Unfriendly fire singed them.
I slide down a few rungs. And I hear that Baghdad has fallen
and several fishmongers have rushed into the street to celebrate.
The Americans counted heads. The Assyrians rode away forever
and a clever man has carved every single fish in the Tigris.

THE BATTLE OF DUDDEN HILL

That far off summer of '76 was a freakishly fucking hot one:
a time to remember and treasure, if heat can remain unforgotten.
Many blurry snaps were shot of girls in bikinis and shorts,
men frying eggs on car bonnets, boys blowing bubbles of thought.
And sent to a plant in Dudden Hill, the overtime compulsory,
where they struggled to keep pace with the products of living history.
Women slaved at their benches, developing its minor pages,
stuffing them into envelopes for the usual derisory wages.

Seventy pence an hour was all that a Grunwicks job offered
for sweltering nine long hours a day to fill the boss's coffers;
there was no air-conditioning, you were sacked if you complained;
you needed to visit the toilets, you politely put up your hand.
Many didn't speak English, so there were few other choices
for women with men in low-pay jobs, children needing choc-ices.
Men who'd hoped for better days still needed to pay the rent.
The annual turnover of staff there was around 100 per cent.

One day a spontaneous go-slow brought matters to a head;
some who'd thought they'd bait the boss were on the street instead.
Then girding up her sari, little Jayaben asked them for her cards
and trooped out with her son Sunil into the sun-drenched yard:
"What you men are running here is a zoo, not a place of work,
but a zoo has many creatures, and some of them can hurt.
You think that we are monkeys who will dance upon your fingers.
But you have picked on lions who will eat you up for dinner."

A narrow street, and a rusty gate, and an ordinary factory
staffed mostly by Asian women, amongst them Jayaben Desai;
and an arrogant employer, Mr George Ward, an Anglo-Indian,
who ruled his staff as people he was automatically better than,
expressed his surprise that women should kick up all that fuss
about such things as tea-breaks, equal pay and related stuff
when he could buy another Patel for fifteen quid – or less –
and he sacked those troublemakers who had tried to join Apex.

That might have been the end of it: the end of Chapter Road
but the story that was written there had yet to fully unfold.
At first the women picketed, to show their peaceful intentions,

94

but police dragged them off by their hair, a fact that went unmentioned
in any daily newspapers, until left-wingers got in on the act
and a tale of angry militants was one that could be wrapped;
and the postal workers of Cricklewood refused to handle packets
addressed to Grunwicks sweatshop by owners of instamatics.

Surprising solidarity was found amongst those local banks
who refused to handle Grunwicks account, to interest said "no thanks".
The official labour movement very little interest mustered
when a cop said to Johnny Patel, "I'll kill you, you Paki bastard."
But little by little that curving street filled up with angry pickets,
spies shinned up the lampposts, old ladies peeped through nets
and extra police were drafted in to put down a revolution
predicted by the Daily Mail – and nearby Willesden Junction.

The SPG rehearsed their moves in a handy nearby crescent;
they charged in a wedge-shaped flying V towards an imaginary presence,
retreating to their Transit vans to await the arrival of pickets
caressing chrome insignia, and slipping them in their pockets.
For our numbers they were growing; more arrived each day
to defend the right to unionise and to strike for decent pay;
to try and stop the scabs' coach on its way down to the gate.
One mighty push would win the day, those workers reinstate.

To wander around those little streets is to be ambushed now
by memories of my comrades gone, for it's thirty years ago
when we were young and up at dawn to ride the coaches down,
prepared to push against the cops, prepared to fight unarmed.
Boys and girls up for the crack, we knew that we were right:
we felt that justice might prevail against the tides of night.
We argued in the greasy spoons that lined the Dudden Hill Road,
breakfasted on sausage and beans, our bubble yet to explode.

Dan Wheeler must have been there, in his early twenties prime.
I can see his face before me – he was great around that time;
rushing out to punch somebody for democracy and Gay Pride
before Aids was invented, before Dan went out with the riptide;
and Will in a wine-coloured velvet coat, a pair of old flip-flops
amusing the serious militants in their donkey jackets and socks

as the picket swelled to thousands, spilling to the High Road –
Trades Unionists and students and punks in spiky haloes.

I remember a nervous Robert, the bacon sandwich in his hand,
slurping at a mug of tea, expounding the transitional programme;
but one demand or another, it was all the same thing to me:
I was there for the crowd rush, the amphetamine of solidarity.
Quakers and Friends of the Earth and Indian Worker's Association
and the SWP and the IMG and a large Labour Party delegation
ridiculed by one and all in the days of Sunny Jim Callaghan
for joining a reformist party that couldn't be led by a duller man

who sat in the Palace of Westminster, paid for by union subscriptions
who sent in the cops against us to reupholster his waning convictions
and Anne Devine in her coat so grey, elbowed her way to the fore
linking arms with a pair of blokes who lifted her off the floor
and passed her back, complaining, to tremblingly pull on her mitts,
calling out in her high Derry accent, how she used to throw stones at the Brits.
And the call to link arms went up again, a scab coach rounded the corner.
We pushed and we pushed and we pushed: we couldn't have pushed any harder.

The myths of 1977 were forged around us as we stamped,
advanced towards the lines of cops; our folding, holding ranks
in which you could lose your footing, be carried off in mid-air
kicking around; a baby child whose parents have lifted her
to run along a beach of gold where crested waves are lapping
where yesterday I saw an old black lady's stick a-tapping
and the sea heaved up its breakers, boys, to snap your bones in two,
for our banners they were red and gold, our jackets they were blue.

I helped her to her doorstep at the far end of Cobbold Road
remembering the day of shame when our victory was sold.
"Action from the TUC is like honey on your elbow. You
can see it, you can smell it, but can you taste it? Hell no!"
So said Mrs Desai, but we still let them march us around
while the scab bus sneaked in quietly from nearby Harlesden Town
and a hundred thousand miners marched out of Willesden Green
furled up their flags and disappeared into a pub they'd seen

bellowing out their orders and the songs of Loretta Lynn,
decent enough fellows, sure enough, when it came to getting them in;
and the mighty Arthur Scargill was arrested right on time,
snapped by fifty cameras of attendant Fleet Street slime.
By the end of that day we were beaten, by a leadership betrayed,
not by organisation; by not grasping the games they played.
Thinking a strike could be squarely won by human physical force
when we were just a stage army which politics endorsed.

"You did a good thing," a woman said, stood by the boot of her car.
I walked back up to the High Road. I sheepishly smiled at her
as though God had personally thanked me for such a casual action
taking it away from me somehow and into the realms of fiction.
I became a politician, my every move had been measured,
a calculation of heavenly bliss, aimed to fulfil my own pleasure
as I had in the days of yore before and would again tomorrow.
I'd helped a little old lady, sure, but still I was plunged in sorrow.

That Labour government was tottering. To keep the Tories out
what might have been our victory had been managed into a rout
to satisfy the floating votes of far-away middle England
anxious about law and order, and immigrants … and pensions.
From bitterness to bitterness the strike committee fought on
pitched battles with the hated cops, fights that couldn't be won.
Seven thousand fought them, hundreds were hospitalised.
Mrs Desai and three others staged a desperate hunger strike.

Union boss Tom Jackson threatened postal workers with the sack
to confiscate their union cards if mail they continued to black.
At a Labour Party conference, strikers were warmly applauded;
a patronising irony because these workers had been defrauded.
For the Grunwicks strike committee, it wasn't a joke or a gesture
by some smiling shit of an academic, some temporary investor.
They were only working-class people, taking it as far as it would go
following the encouragement of the Citizen's Advice Bureau.

The committee called a halt to it in July of the following year.
No workers were reinstated, and no lessons learned for the future
except for the courage of women; they're like a dog with a bone

organising your workplace or making ends meet in your home.
Shame on you working-class leaders, your noses stuck in the trough:
you failed the strikers of Grunwicks, you failed us, so fuck off.
I think of the lives of fallen friends, their smiles in fading snapshots
developing slowly under my hand; my memory is a sweatshop.

Socialism is dead as the dust. I've heard it often, I had no reply
for Rob before he stepped off the train, Dan when he said goodbye.
Anne in that flat in Notting Hill Gate, her daughter next-door sleeping
held the air of a woman crucified, a woman sick of her weeping.
Will Webb – that beautiful optimist – looked, in the week that he died,
to some reconfiguration – rainbow stew in the sweet bye and bye.
And I failed to mind the gap between the platform and the carriage
carrying me back to Harlesden clock, bereft of love or marriage.

And it pains me now to think at all, wandering these roads alone
awaiting news of a life's reprieve via e-mail or mobile phone.
I try to piece it together; what we thought and what we believed
in those far-off days of our golden youth, unjustifiably naïve.
The streets are full of younger kids who know nothing about those times;
the area's full of guns now, black boys shot for partying crimes
as their parents wonder what it's all about; as even I'll admit
the times we lived through lived through us, and spat us out like pips.

But those pips may grow an apple tree or fall on stonier ground
and the ringing words of a prophecy remain but empty sounds
echoing around deserted streets long past midnight's silent tolling
boys and girls of yesterday, who should have gone out bowling;
and the wisdom of the ancient lays, sad mutterings of old fools,
tales heard on another's lips, who went to a singing school.
And it doesn't matter much, you say, what happened then or later;
I make this song to be some young fool's tenth hour revelator.

BLACK KAFKA

Nightfall in little Somalia
the internet cafes are lit up
portals into the Museum of the Air
where Black Kafka is browsing late into the evening
a series of bookmarks, thumbnails, letters
from an old friend, a retired mouse
whose squeaking had come to irritate her people ...
pop ups of pop ups, invitations to talk about nothing
where Black Kafka is browsing late into the evening
with an air of satisfaction and purpose
ignoring the lit webcam, shoulder to shoulder
with an Australian and a Czech
pouring out their hearts into the gamelan ether.

Black Kafka was born in the USA
of mysterious insistent parentage.
At four years old he picked up a ball and chain
and ran with it to the swimming pool.
Little is known of what happened next.
Little can be predicted except the continuation of text
and little Black Kafka began to write his right then
in a motel whose yard was full of blowing leaves
blown bulbs of prairie Columbine
tumbleweed, seed catalogues for plants that blew in anyway
from out of town the broken tunes of a fairground.
Black Kafka was born in the USA.

One day a ten-wheeler stopped for gas and cigarettes
and its driver ate a jar of prairie honey
bitter aftertaste of aloe vera
a man with no backbone who had spines on his tongue
and nowhere to go that didn't have the same law
a law he disagreed with, or seemed to
or so it appeared to the youthful figure of Black Kafka.
Next day he wrote his story about the law of the father
and he wrote down his own name on it
a name he had thought of himself
a name he thought of before he thought of the name.

Mealtimes were difficult for Black Kafka.
How much should he eat?
Enough to survive on, enough to grow tall.
Not much out there for a growing boy.
Hey, Black Kafka.
Talking to himself was like talking to a brick wall.
Talking to himself was like nothing at all.
Turning after the sound of an echo, a footfall.

Perceiving the world as a series of concentric circles
he determined that his escape should be vertical.
Up or down, that was the important question.
He pondered it often on his visits to the restroom.
Should he marry? But it was a stupid question. Who?
One day a bee stung him and his head swelled up so huge
he floated away on it, a black weather balloon,
and he floated from the desert to the green pastures.

You sure have got a swell head, mister
excepting it's black, you got a nigger head on.
Black Kafka shot that man with a gun at the end of his finger.
Hey, Black Kafka. You shot him. If ever a man needed insurance
that man's name was called Black Kafka.
Instead he had a headache.
Instead of justice the law was after his hide.
Instead of running he rented the cheapest room he could find
and he paid for it with folding money.
Instead of living in it he stayed on the outside.

A story of the golden time was needed.
A story of how a story came to be a story.
Nobody knew that one, nobody except Black Kafka.
Nobody except Black Kafka knew that story to be a lie.
Nobody except Black Kafka knew why.

Everything in this world is upside down.
Let's see how they like it with their heads in the shit.
The trees are just trees, the trees are not our friends.
Never trust a man with a snakebite for a wrist-watch.
Never trust a woman who is afraid to eat meat.
Never trust a person who never left town.

In the internet cafes of little Somalia
Black Kafka is running his own business on a shoestring.
Each day money is pouring into his bald account.
Each day is another day, each day he is a little richer
and now he sells his secrets to anyone who clicks.
But can they understand them when they've paid their five dollars?
That's not his problem, because he is an artist.
Because he is an artist they trust anything he says.
When the cafes close down he sleeps, dreaming of the old country.
How could he imagine something like that?

I say he is neither a fool nor wise, I say he is himself
a strange man born in the desert somewhere
who didn't choose the path he is on.
Others who would like to say something about him
they don't know what to say, they don't know.
But for old Black Kafka that's nothing, it has always been so.
He was born in that desert a long time ago.

KOI

for Ken Smith

All night the pool of Koi is fed by a gurgling pipe
that runs down the black sluice part of Alan's water feature
under the small leaded window of John the Lodger
soothed by its cistern-like music to sleepy reveries.

The largest is a Chinese of jointed white porcelain armour
clacking to the surface, new fry swimming from his jaws
as his mottled wives skulk under cabbage-lily pads
his yawning mouth bursts up at a criss-cross barrage of nylon
woven to catch a thieving Heron who used to come and
carry off a three-hundred pound fish in its beak-like jaws,
cajoled or repelled by a plastic one-legged guardian
sure to be finished off by the Chinese, once ensnared.

Alan's off out at 3 am to take another fare to the airport.
He's sixty-three years old, lean, a barking fence-post man.
Alright John? You alright mate? You alright in there?
At the weekend he will dig the pool in deeper, rescue the fry
in a milk bottle, poured into a pair of new bathtubs propped
up on either side of the white bench, always a white bench
and the fence it was painted and strengthened all round.

Mrs Shaw does the house jobs, she's spry, out dancing nights
and coming in late with a brief smile at John the Lodger
who watches TV in the extension. Lock up for me would you?
A raised hand, lights out, alone as a handsome red fox
noses up to the glass door and sniffs twice at the pane.
In possession of the garden now, there's little you can do
to stop them running over from the park into your yard
making an unearthly sound, playing for hours in the moonlight.

John the Lodger. What is he doing here? What's it about?
A low rent bogeyman moonlighting as the hunchback in the park.
How come he ended up here, by accident, by mad design
trapped as the fox is not trapped, and not exactly welcome.
John the Lodger, a necessary part of the paying furniture.
He comes of letting people do your thinking for you
and envy of those who live in glasshouses, who can afford to.

Dappled Koi in the moonlight, the thrash of their tails,
knives sharpened under a rock to jump out and slash
the nose of a sniffing fox from the stadium, the stand of trees
at the edge of the dark lands lying anywhere, anywhere
out there, runnels, the gardens we sneak between.

HORNSEY HOUSING TRUST

They arrive in an Audi and park it over nextdoor's kerb.
Marlene and Alicia, all the way from Wood Green, the long way
out through Willesden and god knows where else, because
usually they don't come this far out into the countryside –
Claremont Road, Cricklewood, opposite slated-for-demolition
Hendon Football Ground – to interview a prospective client
for urgent rehousing in a single flat for over forty-fives.

I'm forty-nine years old. I've only just resigned myself
to being over forty-five, now here I am being asked if I'm incontinent.
But we have to ask these questions, Marlene says, leaning
toward me at the dining room table, touching my wrist,
a gold pen poised over her questionnaire; I hope you won't be
offended by this next one: Do you find it difficult at all
to climb a flight of stairs? No, I reply. Two flights? No, that's okay.
Three flights? I could climb three flights of stairs quite easily,
I say, thinking, yes, especially if you were at the top
as we climb up the stairs to look at my temporary room
standing for a moment at the foot of my narrow bed.

Isn't this totally weird, says Alicia, nodding in her beads.
We were talking to somebody like you a minute ago
weren't we Marlene? Another teacher from Essex, a woman
in the exact same circumstances. You'd have a lot in common with her.
But I feel I have a great deal more in common with Marlene.
There's something special about the way she's leaning forward
and the way we are looking at each other and I look
back into her eyes as I answer her questions
which makes me think I could almost say so, there and then.
But the landlady cometh. She stands at the foot of the table –
a small woman from Liverpool, poking her nose in,
smiling and asking her own questions. Everything is their business.
He stays here on the strict understanding it's temporary.

Afterwards we walk outside to look at the pool of Koi carp.
Marlene exclaims joyfully over them, I stand beside her
and admire them too. We are close together, warm in the sunshine
for longer than is strictly necessary. I project my hopes
out through my loving eyes, right into her open heart

that she will indeed rehouse me, not babbling or anything
but just looking at her and smiling – and meaning it
too, with all my heart, as truly as I can in the present circumstances.
I follow them out to the car, chatting about the quickest way
and I wave them off down Claremont Road
as they head off down towards Brent Cross and the North Circular
and I walk inside again, turning in a little on myself
at the pain of Marlene's absence, wanting to be in her arms.

ANYARDS ROAD

for Geoff Mason

What's the point of these return journeys?
Why return beyond the first few times
except to get your bearings in the adult world
or lick your wounds in the birth-place
where all your it started to come and happen and be
and the you you will always remain despite the chime of
your fictions of transformation, is round again
to drop you out of a clear blue sky
back where you started? The question mark is best avoided
in poetry. Anyway, the answer is a simple one, that
there's a density to your impressions of it
which have a special ngth to them, an ngth
you can't find in the thin spiralling fictions which are all
the world and its titanic sufferings can be
for somebody like you, for whom the ripe moment
of setting out might be the only one unblighted by reality.
Anyards you travelled, past the dairy, past the past
under a crescent moon, on a well-paved broken track
measured here and there by nodding bluebells
& clumps of concurring bonnets of the Mistresses Goody
by the lynch-gate at the far corner of the recreation ground
where stuff came faster than you could get it down.
Anyards Road, least popular route to school
the one lacking in puddles, stones and rutted mud
where you first tasted your own lip's blood
now circling back for more of the same salt:
the punishment of destiny, of the buckers of luck
those poor fuckers who could dream on the road
unanchored but failing to quite float. Well, you don't float
not unless you're Muhammed Ali, Jack Kerouac, or Yevgeny Yevtushenko
straight out of Zima Junction with your packet of typed sheets,
your ticket out of there, on the fast train to Moscow
where the real politics, the interesting stuff
begins and ends with your arrival at Spaceportgrad
when you've made yourself into the only outsider in Big Town.
Is Anyards Road going anywhere, anywards?
The sweetshop's till is full of big clanking washers,

dropped pennies are suspended in mid-air,
a lost sentence before the policeman directing traffic
on a busy morning at the far end of Between Streets
is frozen in mid-gesture in my memory,
the very smoke and steam suspended like rags
of when we were scared kids waiting for him to shoo us over.

3

FIREWRITING

(W.B. to his nurse, London, circa 2002)

How beautiful if curved lines were formed within & on
a plate of rare design, of zinc – and at the touch of notes
made patternings of clear inner sound – in musics of light, or fire scripts
each sound a master letter, written out in luminous fire
each inner linkage of a word and script made visible –
and if we spoke as writing, our thoughts already words ...
　　　　ah, then we'd know
　　　　　　　　how thoughts became these words
or those.
　　　　　　"The Towel of Babel."
　　　　　A child goes goo-gaa:
　　　　　　　　　　learns to recognise
and learns to blame another (copying her mother). Language
measures out the whole nine yards
　　　　　　　　　　of wool
whose kitten trail we might have wished to follow
once, so long ago, only to realise it had
no destination
　　　　　　　& even the guilty kitten had wandered off
leaving us to consider ... what?
Language has its semiotic and mimetic aspect
　　　　　　　　　　　yet the organ of our talk
the mind, made letters for its voice; the letter speaks;
its word and marks are one, the patterns of its sound
are electricity, red-current-sparks fired along the axon to trip the waves
of sound: and this device, this glowing plate I speak of
　　　　　　　mechanysical machine –
well, maybe it could help us find our natural script.

Hah! Hah!
　　　　　No more of strangled syntax sweated out
between ruled lines, but everywhere! the all, all one!
　　　　　　　　　　　　　Why,
wasn't the whole creation uttered into being by God?
　　　　　Were not these written marks
　　　　　　　　bound up with the Word which made us all,
we animals who use speech? One lovely word

containing all, all generals and particulars of drawings, paintings,
sculptures, buildings out of granite, buildings
moulded out of air

                  clogging up my memory
as those wooden shoes that workers used to wear, sabots,
were to derail the locomotive of history ... or not, I fear.

                                         Where was I?
Ah! But this machine would fuse each sound to script
as raggedly precise as halves of broken eggshells joined
as opposites are one, are deeply true – each particle of thought
its negative ion – for it's well known by now (by me)
that written language grew out of this celestial notation
of melodies, of the divine –

                        I'm right, I'm right.
                It doesn't come from us, you know
            but from the angels floating out of reach. I mean.
I mean.
            Just listen to the poverty of human speech.

                        *

Which leads me to a further thought, affinities we share, I trust
as the sun and moon are paired, as Romanticism
bears its traces of the baroque. Let me explain!
I can, if you'll allow me to digress and repossess my way.
Ah yes. It all comes back to the symbol, cher image,
(a memento mori)
which is only a form of writing, after all, if you're a symbolist,
whose meaning can be summarised in words
            just as for the medieval allegorists

                              images were signatures,
mere monograms of essence, not the thing itself
in a masquerade mask; and, at the same time, the written script,
the actual black of the words, was not subordinate,
not cast away like dross
once fire images were forged in the reader's mind,
but absorbed, along with the freight they bore, the very patterned
shape –
      and hence the great love, the great pains they took
with type
and the look of a page.   Simple stuff, really:

112

Our own chaste love would be expressed by swans;
their base Venusian couplings by graveyard crows.
        They really scored it into you,
                        they gouged it into your brain!
Inscription, image – the whole double-bind of Christianity,
the triple bind, if you allow for incantations
as they did
                (fill up my water glass, if you would, I grow a little muddy).
Suffice it to say their view of the relations
of script and speech
                        was a complex, divinely underwritten one –
fully comp, I mean, not merely against fire and theft
or accidental damage to another's soul. Indeed, indeed
not only does their whole philosophy rest on this
their inconsistencies
                        are cut of the same water.
                                        What are they?
What? I'll continue till they become apparent, if it please you.
        Meanwhile, back to the romantics, and whatever it
was they owed to the Baroque –
                        Oh and how's the PhD?
Still going? Good.
Don't bother with my stuff, I've been done.

        Your memory's so much sharper, dear, than mine, let alone
that of the average allegorist – fables were for simpletons, after all,
for those who can't remember facts or arguments; all those for whom
no proof is sweeter than a pudding with a child's leg in it –
        Ah! you're so pretty, dusky too;
        you'll get the job I never did, I know it.
Oh please! there's no need to run off in a huff!
                Where was I …
… hmm, yes, on those picture poems they revell'd in.
Didn't they contain, in essence an idea
that changing line-lengths
                        imitating organic form
would also yield the rise and fall of speech? Especially in your great poet
Coleridge, who also thought quite natural storms
could be materialisations
of cosmic reverberations.
                        Only John Donne, it seems, held
trepidation of the spheres to be quite innocent. Goethe?

Goethe? Schmerter!
Yes, I know, it all came back in him, or never went away,
that classical sense of the interconnectedness of higher and lower forms
(guess where we Jews were placed!)
and of being's intractable Granny knot
which even the blockhead emperor, Marcus Aurelius
fancied he could unravel, unpicked it in his tent at night
in fumbled Greek – and off to slay a few Sarmatians
after light nocturnal anguish
                              (how that Centurian's armpits stank)
after breakfasting on honey.
                              Let's hope this skein of wool
might be something you could cats-cradle
between the verbal and visual manifestations of the baroque:
its teeny-bop horror shows, the clunky mix of metres
jammed together in those naff old German plays
                              'that had to be set up fifty ways'
whose high and low were oft chained up in clink,
(not often changing places though)
whose Jesus walked in carrying a great armful of bones;
angel faces turned deathsheads, rosy cheeks urn-grey.

                              ⋆

You like this stuff? Because of your tender years, no doubt.
          Even your sex might fit you for consideration
of the body in its non-purified aspect, its frangibility, its stench,
its death-like sheddings. Oh, and don't tell me again
I'm in good shape for my age – let's keep it light, my sweet –
but I expect you'd like the way they cut the booty up
and made it weep
                    and seep
so openly with blood:
                         it was because they hated it
they thought it necessary to sacralize it that way –
by dismemberment made far fitter than as a living whole
as which sensuous entity it can be no symbol but itself;
          whereas once they had it in bits
they could pull the sacred from the profane
like a rabbit from an inverted top hat. In those vivid, nasty emblem books
all the charnel house remains

114

became a floating box of severed symbols
whose true meanings were revealed, written and ordained
in fragments
                    somewhat like the clues
in a plotless pseudo-antiquarian detective book
some gallery of stumps and stars
                                I wouldn't wish be seen dead in.
Yes, the medieval emblematists had a penchant for clichés.
In the Tragic Dramatists
                    there's a certain torsion
from lashing up the borrowed bobs and bits.
                                Dealers of death-cards
for whom the glory of your hair would signify
your many and varied thoughts, my dear;
your fine head, your breasts, your large ribcage
your magnanimity and courage; those magnificent hindquarters
your strength, your rage, your lion's roar.
                                I daresay
they would sooner celebrate the chastity of Agatha.
Her undecayed birth-member in the grave – for only
martyrdom could fit a female body to be emblematic:
            your physical pain was useful grist to a plot-mill.
Agatha carried her breasts in on a tray
                        thus became
patron saint of bell ringers, clochards
                        & bakers of small round loaves.

Those jokers viewed the mind-body split as absolute. Rene
Descartes dualism
was about as baroque as his stolen thought antique
and anything like a theory of the passions
has a stinging smack of the medieval mind;
whose spirit is always drifting upwards
while physical bodies stay home & sweat their lice.
There, I told you. So.
For the dramatist of the baroque, a torturer yields
a firmer base for audience emotion
than all of Aristotle's tragic conflicts, added to which,
            they obviously liked to watch.
Compared to rape, dismemberment
                        & flaying women's flesh

arousing fear & pity in respect of a toff's tough break
was a chancy business at the late medieval kiosk.
Then as now, I think you'd find it so
                                        if not I won't quarrel.

          But once you had a corpse to play with
the fun of allegorisation could begin. Off a king in the first five minutes
then you've got something.
                              Oh. I sound like him?
Sorry, sorry. That definitely, definitely won't happen again.
          Death needs time for what it kills to grow in, yes?
Allegorisation can only be carried through in respect of a corpse.
Characters die in order to enter
the world
of allegory: it's transparent.
                              Your immortality's a bagatelle, my sweet,
                    my little bag of chocolate fudge –
compared to your value as dead meat.

                              ★

'He leaves his body as a pledge of his goodwill.'
                                        Oh yes,
and there's a few limp fivers left in the till.
                                        For,
seen from the obscene point of view of death
a corpse gives birth,
decaying flesh falls off, and that which was so purified
comes into its own – dead matter melts away to leave
the purified remains; a naked spirit rises
                                        and what's left
in memory takes on a new life of its own ...
                                        Flies, flies.
I'll open a window, dear. I don't know how they got in. I'm
not that far gone. Could you kill the little fuckers for me?
Paris-Soir. That's favourite, if you wouldn't mind.

                              ★

          I hate to bring up the subject of nakedness, dear.
So did the writers of the baroque. When they did they liked

to leave a nasty taste in your mouth.

                                   Only in the beyond do the blessed
enjoy incorruptible flesh & reciprocal pleasure
in complete purity. Venus stripped her admirers,
so their crime of lust lay unconcealed. Bacchus was naked
because drunks can't keep secrets
or throw away their possessions – here, take my hat, my suit,
I wasn't really enjoying wearing it.

                              They demonised the ancient gods
recommending pious mortification to the flock –
& statues of idols were juxtaposed with dead men's bones
banished from memory to remember their ideas.
Does this remind you of anything ? No? No?
Wait till someone's run off with your clothes, another struts
around, more arrogant than ever, spouting half-baked ideas
you threw off for the price of another package of cigarettes
whose smoke vaporised in an atmosphere of denunciations
where counter-accusations carried no weights.

              I exaggerate?

                              Try surviving on what I did. Yes. Yes.
All your complaints are disallowed by parasites you've harboured
preparing one last feast on your flesh

                              as they wait for you to go down.
Tenured racists strut around the States:
World Authorities on Humanism.

                         That bastard Adorno
had me tethered to a pauper's desk and wrote his name
on my ideas, the ones he stole, corrupted.
I was so naive in those days, had no choice to be otherwise.
Had to be to pay the rent on crumbs from Institutes.

                                   I'm an old-fashioned sort.
Transience, eternity ... confront each other in me
the death-mask of my messianic youth, my middle-age, a fate
in the camps I was lucky to escape

                         on the lost border of flight
when the little hunchback tampered with my revolver.

                                   My writing
stopped right there.

              Blood in the milk & milk in the ink

                              & like
the Angel

of History (a dead man's trope, if ever there was one)
I had to watch in silence (the price of my survival, it seemed)
as the whole murderous play was played: singed, broken wings
not caught in a wind from paradise
but in the breath of hell; my mouth open in a silent scream;
struggling to close my eyes
                              my broken ribs
hanging through cooked flesh.
                              Rat armies gnawed there. O yes I rambled.
Broken shoes, a cardboard suitcase containing an old suit,
a bone comb, a book I'd read a hundred times & one I'd written
                    & I became the nameless one
the sailor without papers
                              who signed up on THE DEATH SHIP
as a stoker in the black gang – trying to find some Poland,
some dump long gone; my Berlin childhood, my ... who? what?
my life happened
not to have happened – not to me, not to anyone.

When they opened up the camps I watched it on the big screen
somewhere in Italy, believe it or not, holed up for two years
in the turfed cesspit
of a country cottage owned by the Ginzburg family,
                              Socialistes de salon, but kind
'That girl of ours will end up marrying a gas-fitter.'
                    That lot seemed to go on skiing right through it.
Ben and La Clara
            by the heels
                    a Milano.
Old Ez in his cosy Pissant cage –
                    they should have strung up the old shit with them.
                    Or turned him on a spit. The Unwobbling Pivot.
Big tattooed eyes
                    shovelled onto trucks, into open pits ...
that was us, that dumped out gone off moon sausage meat.
                                        Black bread,
an ear of mildewed corn between ten thousand of us.
                    Do you hear me? Do you hear?
With your mildewed ear
                    of corn?

                         ★

Ah! thanks for the chocolates! I'm feeling satanic this afternoon.
I'm ready to initiate you into more forbidden knowledge
though how you've never heard of it's a mystery – and a boon.
Life's a chocolate caramel.

                        Perhaps you'd like to chew it for me.
I used to like those ones in the mauve foil, the way
they were always the same all the way through. To tell you the truth
I'm more for surfaces than kernels.

There, I knew you were a kind girl, really.

        Ever heard of Josephine Baker?
        The Queen of the Jungle. I was in the front row.
                Now,
of course, you can get it all on CD.
        Except the stuff I liked
                    The Ooompah Jazz for Whites.

                     *

            Socrates said that knowledge of the good
makes good actions; and Aristotle built his Ethics round it,
happiness, good ways, politics. All bullshit, I'm afraid.
Truer of the knowledge of evil that shines forth in the night
of mournfulness with a subterranean phosphorescence
glimmering from the depths …
                  baroque polymathy
was knowledge of the Black Arts, the Manichees, Astrology.
Demons are so-called by their knowledge, said Augustine;
who should've known this, he went through the whole lot,
refuted them on his way to the cross.
                How could his friend so-and-so
whose diplomatic career carried him far along the whitened roads
be said to share the fate of a Josie Nobody, the fifteenth
daughter of an Alexandrian slave, born on the same date?
How could a fig possibly scream when you plucked it?
Even if it was occupied by the Holy Spirit. It had no mouth.
The Holy Spirit had bigger fish to fry.
                    That sort of rubbish –
the Midas touch that lends significance to everything
and kills it.

                     *

I used to dabble in that sort of thing myself
for some reason it attracted me
being part of what was concealed, of non-official knowledge,
obliterated traces told you what they thought
the people, the people –
                              I thought it highly possible, I wanted
to rescue whatever had failed and sunk
into the dank downworld
                              the Sargasso sea where human sports
and wrecks are stored.
                              All there, all there in the German baroque:
a contrast of high and low, the former aspiring to aether,
the latter struggling through – say what you like about me
my dear, my dear child: I knew which side I was on.
                              I thought the way it all shaped up
this mundane fantastical I loved was
feminine, of the female body,
of the world of the Parisian street women,
what such a woman remembered or forgot
or passed on to her daughter.
                              I see you shake your head.
You're quite right, my dear.
                              Quite right.
        Light the fire, could you?

                              *

                              Could you look
inside the wardrobe there and pass me my dressing gown?
I swapped the Paris silk for the English wool.
                              It's so itchy here!
Got sick of the place at the finish – Sartre's pompous rhetoric,
        Paul Celan getting ready to join his mother
        in the Seine's black soup.
        Mutter, mutter. STAR.
        (I told him to ignore that German shit:
        a tough circuit to crack
        his guilt-loop
        a Moebius strip –
        to forget is to betray, to remember
        exploitation, travesty.)

I always thought
he looked like a conjuror –
                            the too beautiful eyes, the smile,
the nothing up my sleeve
                    except for Sylvia.
            For me it had been almost everything
        that tiger's leap
onto the gazelle of memory
                            (not you, my dear!)
        to drag your formerly darting prey
        through the strait gate of the NOW.
                                I ran away again
when sixty-eight didn't pan out –
            if I lifted up a paving stone
                        I'd want to find more than sand.
Your beautiful hands. So strong and brown, like Jeanne-Marie's.
            You know, I like that child's poems
even more than I used to – are they so complex? prefiguring everything?
or just the lights a shattered glass reflects
as an American
poet sang
        of the Sermon on the Mount?
Anyway, they count as much – or more to me now
than any cynical flâneur. I liked Guy Debord
just couldn't see late capitalism
as he described it, balanced out in clauses of Hegelian rhetoric.
I'd have wanted to upset the flow (too much swept away by it)
        moi aussi
                J'ai fumé de l'eucalyptus.
And I'm still drinking the ragpickers' wine.

                        ★

The purely material & absolutely spiritual
are banner poles of the satanic realm. The guilt of the allegorical
observer, the so-called melancholic (me) is ...
... is that he betrays the world for knowledge.
Guilt.
        The House That Guilt Built.
                        The Tabernacle of Terror.

                        ★

Sometimes I wonder what could possibly have interested me
about allegory.

        I expect it came from a desire to obliterate my own past,
to get a job in the German academy –

            much good it would have done me

            oh my dear, my dear –

            I know you hate it, that's why I do it; my revenge
on your more unlovable aspects, which I doubt that time will purify
or purge of their actual meanings. Ah well, it's all for now,
as well you know. Well, isn't it?
Mien liebe lip?

            I'm no god, but I feel I should be,
fallen into an alien world, become evil, become a creature
sitting next to you with the deadness of a figure, an
abstraction from the pantheon

                in a world of magical, conceptual beings
which is all we are to each other ...

             if I said
I was still up for it, you'd think me like Giotto's cupid –
an ancient demon of wantonness with bat's wings, claws.
And you'd be right, my dear. I'm twisted and skinny now

        still harping on

            like an old saw.

*

Nobody knows the trouble I see. I'm tired, tired of light.
Nobody knows but Jesus. Christ.

        Redeemer of the stories of the small.

        Nobody.

*

            'Weeping we scattered the seed
on the fallow ground and sadly we went away.'

                Evil's only an allegory.
Wherein it means something different than what it is.
Wherein it means precisely the non-existence of what it presents.
The absolute vices of intriguers and tyrants are allegories.
Not real ...

        You look quite puzzled.

Jesus, Jesus.
I must've been a young fool
a right tool
when I thought that.
I did mean something by it though,
something good, perhaps. My thought was only that
what these crimes represent
exists only in the subjective view of melancholy –
they are that view, the vanishing point
and destination of inwardness. What else
is there
to brood about?
Evil is a subjective phenomenon.
The Bible proves it. The Bible
introduces evil in the concept of knowledge,
in the serpent's promise
of knowledge of good and evil.
But God saw everything was good. So:
knowledge of evil has no object.
There is no evil is the world as such, it arises
within man himself with desire of knowledge
which, au fond, is desire to sit in judgement –
to take God's place.
Knowledge of the good
is secondary, it ensues from practice – good ways,
or knowledge of the world. Knowledge of evil
is primary, it ensues from contemplation.
Knowledge of good and evil
is therefore the opposite of factual knowledge – of this or that.
I tell you, it relates to the depths of subjectivity
and is then only really knowledge of evil. It is what Kierkegaard
called 'nonsense', the nonsense of the human heart
in fear and trembling, its unrooted *distensio*.
The baroque sense of evil is quite inadequate, and rooted
in the deficient development of their plots.
I lost mine years ago
distended wanderer, collector of the peasant toys
they made me surrender at every border
starting with that Bavarian three-headed doll of Christ
I remember showing Gershom Scholem; if one head snapped
four eyes still followed you … an obscene name, a living wound, a taunt

123

of the unjust that promises there is no justice
and tells how those who seek it will die.

                            Even here they say no room, no room
no room for clothes peg soldiers, paintings by the damned.
        It's been a long wander down a long street.
                                  Do you know
who you remind me of? Asja, Asja Lacis
                      who spent the revolution
consulting with her dressmaker – but made me a revolutionist
on the isle of Capri.
            I mean it as a compliment.
                         Not that you look
anything like her
        who carved this journey through me.
      Come, come – make haste, my dear,
           I was twenty-one yesterday, I think. Subtract the hundred
      throw away the numbers you're unsure of.
I'm here & now. I'm leaving three centuries behind me.

                         ★

                        Do you know Hamlet?
Of course, of course. To be or not to be

        to me it seems simple
        not existential
        non-referential
        not relating, really
        to the instabilities of
        nascent bourgeois subjectivity
        nor is he made of bits of wood
        nor anagrams for lunch
        nor is he allowed (or rented)
        (je suis permis? je suis loué? ça veut rien dire!)
        au contraire, il a rien à faire
        but remember to forget they killed his father
        comme lui a dit le phantome
        shut up, shut up about it
        and marry the drip
        Ophélie.

                     ★

I began from the object
　　　riddled with error: myself. Ended up here. The city
Rimbaud hated
　　　　　　for its endless dreary Sundays, its fans
　　　of empty terraced
suburbs, the stupidity of their dim inhabitants.
　　　　　　　　　　　　　　When I first came
I winced at the shocking price of gloves in Burlington's arcade.
　　　Tried the East End next.
More like it! I especially liked the docks, as he did
　　　　　　　　　　　all those little streets
like grooves
　　　　where one might lose oneself, skid off
　　　then find the hard dark woods
of the Indies, such as no-one's seen. They made splendid imaginary things
of all that.
　　　　　I especially liked those little bars around the markets
　　　　　　　where you heard
such useless words – les choses blancs –
and strange little animals in their leather cages
sold to all and sundry by the silver men, ces hommes si pauvres, si nets.

But there was something I never understood about that place.

Soho had its charms
　　　　　　(although I was never able to locate them.)
Crouch End had a squat name
　　　　　　　　　Highgate, a tomb. Notting Hill
reminded me of climbing up the steep inclines of Negative Dialectics
　　　(not a trip I've personally undertaken),
an image of the cross -- its allegory of love, of self-negation.
　　　　　　Camden was the box of cogs.
Kilburn – I'd seen a bit too much of that – and
　　　Islington, that thoroughfare of minor beings –
　　　of Islings, quislings, quangos in their paper worlds
　　　　　　　　　　　　　of paltry rhymes:
I is therefore I am
　　　you ain't.
　　　　　　　Highbury was a resting place of Egyptian kings.
Wandsworth the full measure of magic and sex,
　　　　　no more than a dull itch

at the gangrenous shore of Greenwich. O but to be
           done with the respectable town of bricks
of a Silvertown beyond the reach
           of a Knightsbridge you did not want to cross over
to other destinations on a Red Rover.

           Marble Arch reminded me of Heaven
a kind of roundabout to everywhere in town, its villages
of Hell – a park to hide in – a rotting plank, cleaned up – sure ditch –
      the hammering machines of immigrants
in Redchurch Street
           sewing up their own bright shrouds.

                ★

Many men have endured the pain of a Bachelor's Ill Luck;
that special shame of carrying the can home in your left hand
of having no-one's forehead to smite except your own
with your right. I am no exception to that, although
eventually you do come to accept solitude.
Like Franz I didn't really travel much. When I was younger, yes,
but not much recently. (Moscow was my love-trial, all that
counting kopecks for coffee, Asja Lacis unavailable.
I watched revolutionary plays with her husband Stefan George:
his loud German translations, my ad hoc commentary
seemed to rather annoy the Russkies & I found myself trying
to show the proofs of my little book to nobody.
               They left me out of the Great Encyclopaedia,
a nonentity of the Jewish Revolution;
and the war was ditches and charred fields of red clay.)
You know, it takes a life as long as mine
               to try and fail to reach the next village –
you wonder why you came, or went,
your message from a dead emperor doesn't play.
I tended to stay at home, wherever that was, yes,
and curse
the clotheshorse shape-shifter, The Odradek
        of guilt you can't get rid of
or contain.

                ★

I was a sort of frenzied browser
　　　　　　　with a sort of vague plan
To answer the frenzied rape of the Earth
　　　　with a frenzy of procreation
To annex the irrational for revolution
　　　　　To find it in the vertigo of acquisition.
Necessity is the mother of desperation.

　　　　　　　　　Gaga in the Luna Park
my friend Siegfried Kracauer saw the Tiller Girls' high kicks
as akin to those of holidaying factory hands
rehearsing the jerky movements of the production line
producing a sexual liberation
that would liberate humankind.
I have purchased my few groceries at *Flaneur's* Food and Wine
on Holloway Road. (I had to laugh at that.)
and seen the mounted girl legs on a shop sign
performing their mechanical Oxford Street can-can;
and a small hunting bird – un chassagnol – was
talking to a tortoise-head in spats and tails. Who
could choose between the two of them
but that long-billed girl in a cork dress and Waterford crystal heels?
Les fleurs animées; all those dressed up hags
etched and coloured in by Grandville's great city hand.
No conjuring trick could stay the rise of uniforms
or fetishes of violence and of power
that mesmerised our age and yours. Applause:
machine-gun fire
reified, the real bowing actors creased by flying lead.
The world became an intoxicated forcing-house of meanings.
The pleasure of false-connections emptied out all other pleasures.
In my day there was no room for half-measures –
Yes, and no exaggeration that might not prove true a day later;
and every fantastic beast from the Age of Marvels
except the chimera of a working-class victory.

　　　　　　　　　　　*

　　　　　　I don't like myself that much sometimes
but, on the whole, I like me more than what they've made of me.
I'm a ghost, a dense ghost
made of one kind of heavy water.

You can cut me and I bleed thought, stars. Silent soon, but
it seems the smallest speck of me
opens into a thousand universes of still more things to say
and, if the old joints creak a little,
you might almost think I am eternal.
But that thought of mine is of no more value
than as precious, damaged rocks
out of which to carve the future, even less than that
for you, your eyes the colour of marbles (lost)
revealing only
only poverty
                of your version of my century's history.
I return, I return to the only state I cared for much –

The State of Permanent Emergency.

                To be your icon, your mirror, your Walt Whitman eidolon
fixed, unfixed, and rolling on in a long peal of thunder
because you needed me
you need me now and you always will –
I am the trace, the illness and the aspirin
for whose who live in waiting
to whom all things may come. My firewriting, still smouldering
like my eyes, my dear one
                        or yours burst into flame.
                                        Profane illumination –
what was it? A dope-borne apprehension of the mineral
interconnectedness of everything.
                        In Paris, smashed
dear Ernst Bloch's knee seemed an aeon away
yet I felt an irresistible urge to reach and touch it. The surrealist movement,
viewed at its source or from further downstream,
returned the energies of the revolution to sex. But think!
Profane illumination – a wasp buzzing straight into your screwed up
concentrating eye; up you leap in fright –
you can do nothing else, my dear. You bat around;
a madman, striking the air. It's urgent compared to Breton
on New York's Broadway, besieged by butterflies.
Some people get on, as they say, like a house on fire.
And then there's the moment of withdrawal, reeling
yourself in like a bobbin you threw in an excess of carpe diem.

In the future everyone will live in glass houses – but don't
leave your socks out on the garage door to dry.

We're like a child in the panorama who finds the sky too grey
who must be told by his mother
"that's what the weather is like in war".

The world lives on itself: its excrements
are its nourishment.

Without goal, unless the joy
of the circle is itself a goal
Without will, unless a ring
feels good will towards itself –

Thus every tradition becomes, for Nietszche
the legacy of something that has run its course.

All that we seek – love, truth,
These fruits of the sky, fallen on earth's palate …

… Torn from the trees of God's orchards in heaven …

Untasted, without nourishment, spoiled, already rotten.

The experience of our generation
taught that capitalism would not die a natural death.

★

Forgive? forget?
The young are laughing on the streets,
quite happy to be sucked up by the great Wen.
The Great When.
I think it's now, or soon.
Firewriting, ah there was a thing.
Everything else went down like ninepins.
And I mean everything.
Velocity? The giant's toothbrush? Grinning all the way to hell
on a celestial railroad built over the bones of the dead.
White Teeth.
I see one of your lot's written a big book about all that. Too late

to read it now. Too late for tales of those who went or those
who stayed, although I can't see why.

                                        Anyway, let's hear these stories
of those who came to stay. I quite liked … what's his name.

                     You want to wash my face *again*?

        Why? Is the Kaiser coming?
Well, I daresay he'll take us as he finds us, as ever,
if he can still climb up the seven flights of stairs.

                                     Brecht. Yes. Him.
Now he was okay – though not what I'd call one of the Good People.
Not really. Nor am I – a

                        sprucer who blued it,
                 might as well say. Another jab?
                       Excellent!
At least I won't be going back
to that bungalow of ricky-tick

                       up the arsehole of wherever.
Firewriting though.

                  Each sound to be its proper letter.
           I see them jumping now
jumping into a thousand pictures of light, coloured sand icons
on a zinc kaleidoscope, heated by some blue filament
of exceedingly rare design; a harmony-machine;
all the old signs obliterated
in a trice, a touch, a vanishing of dust
yet how we all danced on our clockwork-driven wheel
in the frozen attitudes of a masque of death. Do you see them?
              Do you?
Motes & men.
Of which I had such a strange dream. Last night, this morning, I
dreamed
& dreamed, afflicted as lonely sleepers often are by a great
deal of unseasonable misery —

                     I dreamed everything
             & then forgot to wash
                       & to shave
before telling its story
& now I am marooned forever on these island shores.

Printed in the United Kingdom
by Lightning Source UK Ltd.
103345UKS00001B/211-225